Modern British Jewellery Designers 1960-1980
A Collector's Guide

18ct gold diamond and dioptase geode pendant brooch, by Andrew Grima, 1970

Modern British Jewellery Designers 1960-1980
A Collector's Guide

MARY ANN WINGFIELD

ACC ART BOOKS

Above:
Two-colour gold rhodochrosite crystal pendant by Gilian Packard, maker's mark GEP, 1970

Right:
Citrine and diamond ring in 18ct yellow gold by Hans Georg Mautner, maker's mark HGM, 1970

Contents

06 Foreword by David Armstrong-Jones, 2nd Earl of Snowdon

08 The Art of Collecting

12 Introduction

The Designers

- **20** Frances Beck and Ernest Blyth
- **24** Gerald Benney CBE
- **26** Ingeborg Bratman
- **28** Jocelyn Burton
- **34** Charles de Temple
- **36** Leo de Vroomen
- **42** Stuart Devlin CMG
- **48** John Donald
- **56** Rod Edwards
- **60** Gerda Flöckinger CBE
- **64** Elizabeth Gage MBE
- **68** Alan Gard
- **74** Michael Gosschalk
- **78** Andrew Grima
- **94** Alfred Gruber and Jacqueline Stieger
- **100** Roger King
- **106** Roy King
- **108** Joseph, Paul and Roger Kutchinsky
- **112** Hans Georg Mautner
- **122** David Morris
- **124** Louis Osman
- **126** Gilian Packard
- **132** Wendy Ramshaw CBE
- **136** Ben Rosenfeld
- **142** Tom Scott
- **146** David Thomas
- **152** George Weil

154 Bibliography
155 Acknowledgements

Foreword
by David Armstrong-Jones, 2nd Earl of Snowdon

When Mary Ann Wingfield asked me to write the foreword to this highly researched book she did so knowing of my passion for design but also for the support and encouragement that my parents had given the creative jewellery designers and makers in the 1960s and 1970s. She wanted to press home the point that good jewellery design does not have to be expensive or use materials of great value to make a statement, but it does have to be unusual and different in its definition.

I inherited my love of design from my father, the 1st Earl of Snowdon, who was always fascinated by pushing the boundaries of an object to see where the design potential might end up.

It was he who encouraged my mother, Princess Margaret, to support the creative talent of the independent jewellery designers who were testing the boundaries of new possibilities in jewellery making and design in the early 1960s.

It was he who opened the new jewellery shop in Jermyn Street for Andrew Grima in 1966, and it was he who organised the visit of the Princess and her mother, HM Queen Elizabeth The Queen Mother, to John Donald's mews studio in Bayswater in the 1960s.

Provenance, in the case of jewellery, is particularly important. Each piece has a story to tell and to many people this ranks high in priority when it comes to adding to their collections. In my role as Honorary Chairman of Christie's EMERI, I am fortunate to work with collectors from all over Europe and the Middle East and to help them in their endeavour to acquire or sell the finest works of art, covering over 80 categories including jewellery. When we came to auction the jewellery collection of my mother in 2006, each piece of jewellery was sold with the correct documentation to establish its provenance.

I hope that this book will go some way to expanding the interest in this unique era of British jewellery, when the boundaries of design and craftsmanship were pushed to their limits.

18ct yellow gold open work ring of abstract design set with single-cut diamonds, signed GRIMA, 1968

The Art of Collecting

Whatever they tell you about collecting, it is not cheap. It is costly in time, commitment and research, and that is before you have even purchased the first item in the category you have chosen.

Whatever they tell you about collecting, you would be wise to make a budget and to keep to it. Otherwise, your enthusiasm will run away with you and your money.

Whatever they tell you about collecting, be warned that it can become addictive and needs strict boundaries to be kept under control.

Whatever they tell you about collecting, an impeccable provenance for all the items in your collection should be your ultimate aim.

Whatever else they tell you about collecting, remember to have fun!

I am a collector of wearable art in the form of jewellery designed and made in the UK during the 1960s and 1970s. I do not collect for the value of the metal or the stones used but for the artistry of the designer who created the piece.

All the jewellery I collect is signed by the designer and/or the maker; it is also UK assay marked with the quality of the metal and date stamped, as collectors like to know as much as possible about the jewellery they own.

The jewellery designers and makers working in the UK during the 1960s and 1970s were great artists and craftsmen – men and women who would never sacrifice standards or quality. This attention to detail extended to the boxes they made for their jewellery. Sadly, over the years, the original boxes have become very scarce, as have the receipts.

I am passionate about keeping – or trying to find – the original boxes for each piece I collect. For collectors, boxes and receipts add to the provenance of the jewellery, which is of great importance after it becomes vintage.

With regards to investment, knowing the provenance of a piece adds hugely to its value over time. As such, I would strongly urge collectors of contemporary jewellery to think twice before chucking boxes and receipts out with the rubbish.

HRH Princess Margaret is a good example of a great collector. She was meticulous about keeping her designer jewellery in its individual boxes. When her personal collection came to be sold in 2006, four years after her death, every piece had been carefully recorded and had a story to tell. Provenance could be established, which greatly added to the value.

A platinum, diamond and fantasy-cut aquamarine pendant by Andrew Grima, 1973. The aquamarine was cut by innovative lapidary Bernd Munsteiner

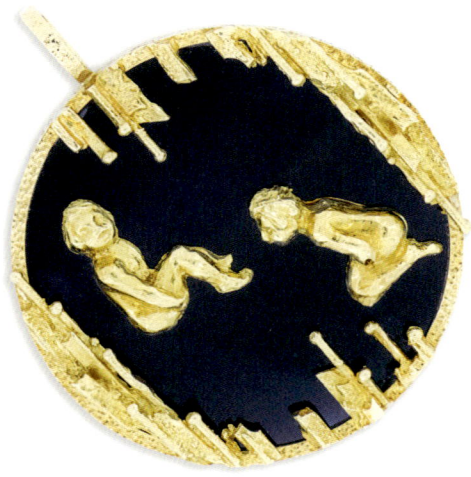

Above:
Faceted citrine and 18ct gold ring, by Frances Beck and Ernest Blyth, 1970

Left:
Black onyx and 18ct gold 'Gemini' pendant, by Kutchinsky, 1964

Right:
18ct gold, sapphire and diamond brooch, by David Morris, 1970

Introduction

Anyone who is interested in twentieth-century jewellery will have their own views on the greatest designers working in the UK in the 1960s and 1970s. Most, however, agree that the outstanding star was Andrew Grima, followed by John Donald, David Thomas, Alan Gard and Gerda Flöckinger.

Four of these jewellers, along with Hans Georg Mautner, Gilian Packard and Rod Edwards, exhibited at the International Exhibition of Modern Jewellery 1890-1961, a groundbreaking event organised by Graham Hughes,[1] Art Director of The Worshipful Company of Goldsmiths (1961-1981), in association with the V&A Museum, London, which encouraged jewellers to push boundaries in design.

It is impossible to overestimate how important this exhibition was because it revitalised a moribund and stagnant industry, that of the independent jewellery craftsmen, who could not find a market for their work at home. The exhibition, held at Goldsmiths' Hall in 1961, showed 901 jewels from 33 countries. To coincide with the exhibition, De Beers, the famous diamond company, launched a competition to find great jewellery designers, offering prize money of £10,000.

As a result of the exhibition, the nucleus of a permanent jewellery collection at Goldsmiths' Hall was formed by gift, bequest and purchase. The collection includes two brooches by Alfred Gruber, who did not contribute to the exhibition, but whose exceptional work, like many other designers in this book, deserves to be brought to wider public attention.

To understand the revolution of jewellery design in the early 1960s, we need to set the scene. The exhibition in 1961, and the competitions that followed, were undoubted game changers, but the reduction of purchase tax to a more affordable level in 1960 and the "pegging" of the gold price in 1961 were similarly important.

The dreaded purchase tax, which was introduced in October 1940, was a complicated consumer tax levied on the wholesale value of luxury goods sold in the UK. One of the problems with the tax was that there were varying rates for different goods. Mink coats and jewellery, for example, were levied at a far higher rate than office requisites. It made purchases of new jewellery totally unaffordable, so not much jewellery was made and sold between 1940 and 1960.

The tax was originally designed to prioritise essential raw materials which were needed in the Second World War, but after the war successive governments obviously thought that they were on to a good thing. Purchase tax ran at various rates, from 33.5 per cent to an eye-watering 125 per cent (1951/1952), until 1973 when the name was changed to Value Added Tax, which is still with us today. The difference is that now the tax is levied on all goods at the point of sale and at a more affordable level of 20 per cent, albeit with a few exceptions.

By 1960,[2] the rate of purchase tax had reduced to 25 per cent for the highest level of luxury goods which, undoubtedly, helped to turn the tide in favour of goldsmiths and jewellery designers. By then, even the most optimistic must have realised that purchase tax was here to stay, in some form or other, as a permanent feature of the taxation system, and the best thing to do was to get on and accept it.

In November 1961 goldsmiths were given another boost. The London Gold Pool was formed by eight central banks in the USA and seven European countries to "peg" the price of gold at $35 per ounce. It remained pegged until 1968 when the London Gold Pool collapsed because gold, at such a low price, could not be sustained. As a result, the price of gold immediately shot up to $40 per ounce until, finally, it forced the collapse of the convertibility of gold, under the Bretton Woods System in 1971.

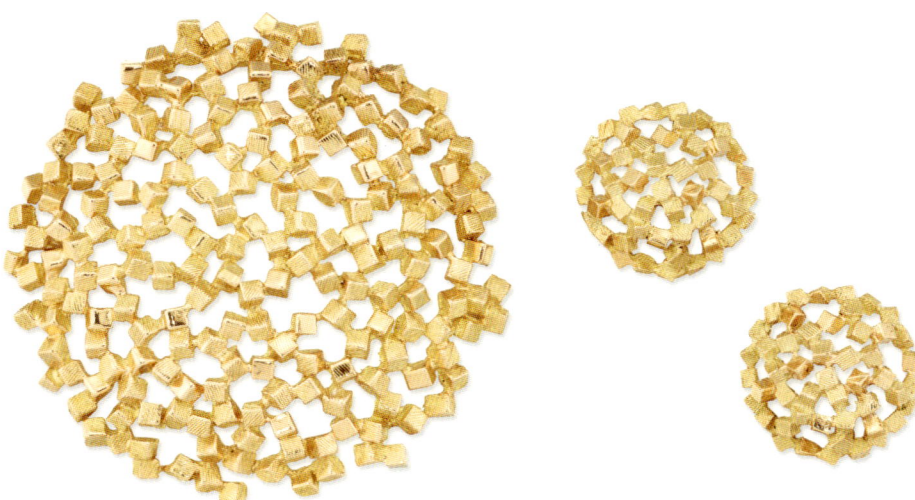

Brooch and earrings in 18ct striated gold cubes by John Donald, maker's mark JAD, earrings 1968, brooch 1969

From then on, things were never quite the same for goldsmiths. For example, on 21 August 2019, the price of gold was fluctuating on the week from £1,231.01 to £1,264.05 per ounce – a swing of 1.16 per cent. On 22 August 2020, the price had increased to £1,460 per ounce on the week.

Did the independent goldsmiths and jewellery designers working throughout the 1960s realise how fortunate they were to be able to buy gold so cheaply; did they even realise that it was cheap? Some of them clearly did because both John Donald[3] and Elizabeth Gage[4] mentioned it in their books and Donald, in particular, made a great deal of his jewellery in the 1960s in 18ct yellow gold, using his famous striated cube or nugget flake designs, with minimum use of precious stones.

The Design Centre Awards were initiated in 1956 to encourage creative design in industrial products. In 1959, the awards Chairman, HRH the Duke of Edinburgh, offered his own prize, the Duke of Edinburgh's Prize for Elegant Design, which was won in 1966 by Andrew Grima with a collection of 15 pieces of precious jewellery, chosen by the select panel, made by his HJ Co. Ltd. This is the only time (thus far) that jewellery has won the prize.

Her Majesty The Queen has one of the 15 winning Grima pieces – a brooch – in her personal collection of jewellery, presented to her by the late Duke of Edinburgh. (Where in the world are the other pieces?) She wears it quite often; indeed, she can be seen wearing it in the diamond wedding photographs of her and the Duke of Edinburgh, taken in 2007.

If the early 1960s was all about the emergence of a new school of creative design in Britain's jewellery industry, then the rest of the decade was about selling the new designs abroad. To that end, the indefatigable Graham Hughes worked tirelessly with an assistant and usually four or five designers, backed by The Worshipful Company of Goldsmiths and the British Board of Trade, to man trade stands, department store promotions and shop windows in places as far away as Tokyo and the USA, persuading shopkeepers to buy British designer jewellery.

The home market was flat. The 1960s London fashion scene was all about adolescence. The primness of the 1950s, with its twinsets and pearls, was cast aside in favour of the miniskirt (synonymous with Mary Quant), which dominated women's fashion from 1964 onwards. Legs were now encased in tights,[5] a new product which really revolutionised the fashion scene. They were liberating and made the possibility of miniskirts a reality, which spelt freedom to a new generation of women.

Whilst tights were enthusiastically embraced, first by the super models, then by the young, and, later, by everybody else, it took until the 1970s for tights to overtake stockings in popularity and for pantyhose, as they were known less glamorously at the time, to become a wardrobe staple. The Swinging Sixties had arrived and for women it was all about burning their bras and the dreaded Playtex girdle, with its suspenders attached to stockings. Mary Quant (Bazaar) and Barbara Hulanicki (Biba), with their quirky designs, influenced fashion, and the flat-chested, long-legged super models Twiggy[6] and Jean Shrimpton[7] inspired the adolescents. Except for the paper and plastic jewellery made by Wendy Ramshaw for Mary Quant's Bazaar, and the enamel pieces made by Gerda Flöckinger for the same store, not much designer jewellery was sold in Britain. That would come later, in the 1970s and 1980s, with power dressing and the growing confidence of women to buy their own jewellery.

In 1977, The Worshipful Company of Goldsmiths celebrated their 650th birthday (1327–1977). Apart from cake and champagne, they marked the occasion with an exhibition of jewellery and silver entitled Explosion. This was again curated by the ever energetic Graham Hughes, who was still Art Director at Goldsmiths' Hall.

The exhibition was particularly interesting because it showcased the important progress that British designer jewellery had made since the 1961 exhibition that Hughes had launched at Goldsmiths' Hall. Explosion showed that the number of jewellery pieces now owned by the Hall at least rivalled the number of pieces of silver, which had played a far more important role than jewellery in the 1950s and early 1960s.

People often ask if there was an identifiable style for the 1960s and another style for the 1970s, thereby defining the two decades by distinct periods. The 1960s was the decade when experiments with gold took place. Andrew Grima brought textured surfaces to ring shanks and brooches; fused gold to gold to produce gritty surfaces; and drizzled molten yellow gold over stones. Gerda Flöckinger brought bold experiments with fused metals, silver and gold. John Donald introduced his gold striated cubes and nugget flakes. It led Donald to remark: "I felt sorry for the designers following us, ten years later, as we had all experimented in so many ways that they found it difficult to be innovative."[8]

The 1960s was also the decade in which designers used natural stones for their jewellery. Graham Hughes has credited Nevin Holmes' 1960 silver ring, made using an uncut opal, with being, "Probably the first modern jewel ever made in Britain using a rough as opposed to polished stone."[9] Coloured stones began to be popular in the form of tourmalines, fire opals and dioptase.

If the 1960s was the decade of new beginnings, experiments and exports from the small collection of independent jewellery designers and makers who were busy establishing themselves, then the 1970s was the decade that definitely majored on those early successes. The 1970s also saw the rise in popularity of unusual cuts in stone, perfected by the stone cutters of Idar-Oberstein, Germany, in particular the house of Munsteiner. Yellow gold continued to be fashionable, and faux pearl necklaces were popular, typically worn as long strands, in layers or as a choker. Jewellery designers like Charles de Temple majored on this trend. Cuffs, bangles and bracelets were all in vogue, the larger the better.

Patronage is so important, and the royal family played a hugely important role in supporting independent jewellery designers and makers early in the 1960s. HRH Princess Margaret numbered many of the leading jewellery designers in her collection, which

Jean Shrimpton wearing an Andrew Grima aquamarine on the cover of *Vogue*, 1965

Above:
The Prince of Wales' Investiture Coronet from 1969, by Louis Osman. Gold, platinum, diamond and emerald with purple velvet and an ermine Cap of Estate. Image courtesy of The Royal Collection Trust

Following pages:
Diamond and ruby-set brooch and earclip suite, 18ct gold, maker's mark Kutchinsky, 1963

was auctioned by Christie's in 2006, four years after her death. On 6 May 1960 Margaret married the photographer Antony Armstrong-Jones (created 1st Earl of Snowdon in 1961), who was interested in design himself and encouraged her interest in the creative talents of British jewellery designers.

The goldsmith Louis Osman was commissioned by The Worshipful Company of Goldsmiths to create the only known British royal crown to be made in the twentieth century, which was worn by HRH Prince Charles on his investiture as Prince of Wales in 1969. It is an interesting work, since the body of the crown is made in 24ct Welsh gold and iridium, a noble metal not normally used in jewellery.

Then, in 1979, just when everything was going so well for the goldsmiths and silversmiths, the price of silver (manipulated by the infamous Bunker Hunt brothers) shot from $6 per ounce to a record high of $48.70 per ounce, before collapsing on 27 March 1980 (thereafter known as "Silver Thursday"), threatening to bring down the entire American financial system in the process and making a number of high-ranking individuals bankrupt. Many British craftsmen felt the impact of this event.

Between January and March 1980, jewellery company Tiffany & Co. ran a series of furious advertisements in the *New York Times* attacking silver hoarders for their greed and selfishness in causing misery to so many people. No names were mentioned but, of course, everybody knew who the silver hoarders were.

Many British craftsmen, particularly silversmiths, also felt the impact of this event. It led Stuart Devlin to remark sagely that "you learn more on the way down than you do on the way up".[10]

By the end of 1980, Graham Hughes was looking for a new direction in his life and one that did not involve the Worshipful Company of Goldsmiths. He resigned in 1981, and devoted the next 29 years of his life to the arts and writing.

With his departure it seems an appropriate time to close a remarkable era in the promotion of modern jewellery and precious metal making. Hughes had helped to turn the drab pessimism of post-war Britain into a hotbed of innovative design. The halcyon days were over but the flowering of creativity that Hughes and the exhibition of 1961 had launched would be remembered for ever.

---

1. Graham Hughes, born April 1926, died November 2010.
2. *Hansard Parliamentary Debates*, 6th ser., vol. 620 (1960), cols 148-53.
3. John Donald and Russell Cassleton Elliott, *Precious Statements: John Donald, Designer and Jeweller* (Carmarthen: McNidder & Grace, 2015), 249.
4. Elizabeth Gage and Fleur Cowles, *The Unconventional Gage: A Book of Unique Jewellery Design* (London: New Gate Press, 2003), 14.
5. First invented by Allen E. Gant in 1959.
6. Dame Lesley Lawson, DBE, born 19 September 1949.
7. Jean Shrimpton, born 7 November 1942.
8. Donald and Cassleton Elliott, *Precious Statements*, 36.
9. *Explosion*, catalogue for the 1977 exhibition held at Goldsmiths' Hall, see Nevin Holmes.
10. Carole Devlin and Victoria Kate Simkin, eds, *Stuart Devlin: Designer, Goldsmith, Silversmith*. (Woodbridge: ACC Art Books, 2018), 446.

THE DESIGNERS

Frances Beck / Ernest Blyth
1939-2021 / 1939-1995

Frances Mary Beck worked for Andrew Grima in the 1960s and whilst she was there, she met Ernest Blyth. The pair formed a joint workshop in 1966.[1] Beck and Blyth are probably better known as a team than they are for their individual work.

Ernest Alexander Blyth, who was English, studied silversmithing at the Central School of Arts and Crafts, London, from 1957 and went on to work as an apprentice assayer at Goldsmiths' Hall in 1961. Beck, who was Scottish, studied at the Glasgow School of Art.

In his early days, Blyth was influenced by the work of Georg Jensen and, more specifically, by the Danish designer, Henning Koppel, who worked for Jensen in the mid-twentieth century. Blyth created a range of Modernist-inspired brooches during the 1960s for Ivan Tarratt of Tarratt's jewellery shop in Leicester (see page 22). Like Georg Jensen, Tarratt worked with leading jewellery designers of the day to develop an in-house collection.

During the 1960s, Beck and Blyth were making waves. In October 1967, they were mentioned in the *Financial Times* amongst four of London's up-and-coming young jewellery designers exhibiting in Brussels that week. The other designers were Gilian Packard (see page 126) and Peter Hauffe.

Graham Hughes, Art Director of The Worshipful Company of Goldsmiths, was also a fan of the talented pair, acting as their mentor. In a promotional leaflet on Beck and Blyth, issued by Goldsmiths' Hall in November 1968, 21 pieces of their jewellery appear in black and white photos. Interestingly, none of them are in the Jensen style so loved by Blyth. The accompanying caption to the photographs is a quote from Beck and Blyth, which reads: "Most of the jewellery which we produce is the result of an initial idea of either one of us, but as a result of discussion, suggestion and criticism, the completed piece is often in fact a joint work. We have, however, distinct individual styles – Ernest tending to design bolder pieces and Frances designing lighter, almost frothy, pieces."

Both designers won a De Beers Diamonds International Award in 1968. When Blyth died in 1995, Beck stopped making jewellery and returned to painting and printmaking. Examples of Beck and Blyth's work can be found in the Aberdeen Art Gallery, the National Museum of Scotland, Edinburgh, the V&A, London, and in the permanent collection of The Worshipful Company of Goldsmiths at Goldsmiths' Hall, London.

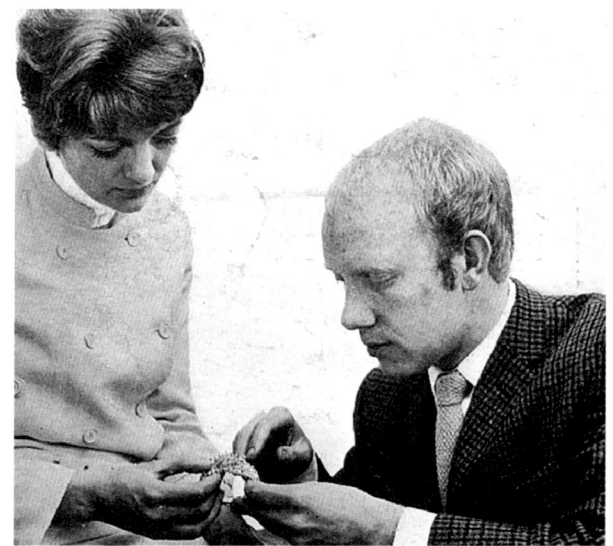

---

1. *Goldsmith Guide*, November 1968.

18ct gold starburst brooch with a cluster of marquise-cut aquamarines, with brilliant-cut diamonds, Frances Beck, maker's mark FMB, 1969

9ct gold bar brooch, signed Ernest A. Blyth, made for George Tarratt Ltd, 1964

"WE SHARE A FASCINATION FOR THE IMMENSE POSSIBILITIES IN THE WORKING OF GOLD, AND ARE PARTICULARLY INTERESTED IN SURFACE TEXTURES... WE BOTH FEEL THAT A PIECE OF JEWELLERY SHOULD BE SUFFICIENTLY BOLD TO CREATE AN IMMEDIATE IMPACT, BUT, AT THE SAME TIME SHOULD BE RICH ENOUGH TO SUSTAIN THE MYSTERY WHICH WE CONSIDER TO BE ESSENTIAL TO ALL JEWELLERY."

Frances Beck and Ernest Blyth

Gerald Benney CBE
1930-2008

Adrian Gerald Benney was one of the most influential British goldsmiths of the twentieth century and the first British craftsman to hold four Royal Warrants simultaneously, during a career spanning more than 50 years.

Born in Hull, East Yorkshire, his father became principal of Brighton College of Art, which Benney attended between 1946 and 1948. He went on to study at the Royal College of Art where he met the designers and silversmiths, David Mellor and Robert Welch, and the jeweller John Donald (see page 48), with whom he shared his first studio, off Tottenham Court Road. Influenced by modern Scandinavian design, Benney and his colleagues went on to revolutionise post-war silver design.

In 1968, in Zürich, Benney met the enameller, Berger Bergersen, who worked for the house of Burch-Korrodi. He had previously worked for Carl Fabergé's great rival, W.A. Bolin. Benney, wanting to develop the use of enamel to further embellish his silver objects and design, persuaded Berger to come to England to train up his workshop in the art of enamelling.

In 1969, Benney moved his London studio to Falcon Wharf, Bankside, and later to Bear Lane, Southwark. In 1971, he was awarded Royal Designer for Industry, and from 1974 to 1983 he was professor of silversmithing and jewellery at the Royal College of Art. He was awarded a CBE in 1995.

Right:
18ct gold and diamond ring, engraved swirl decoration, maker's mark AGB, 1979

Opposite:
Pendant in 18ct gold, cast and pierced, set with 20 small topaz and 5 small peridots, with large central topaz, 1961; this brooch won third prize at the De Beers British Jewellery Competition 1961, in the section for items worth up to £750. Collection: The Worshipful Company of Goldsmiths

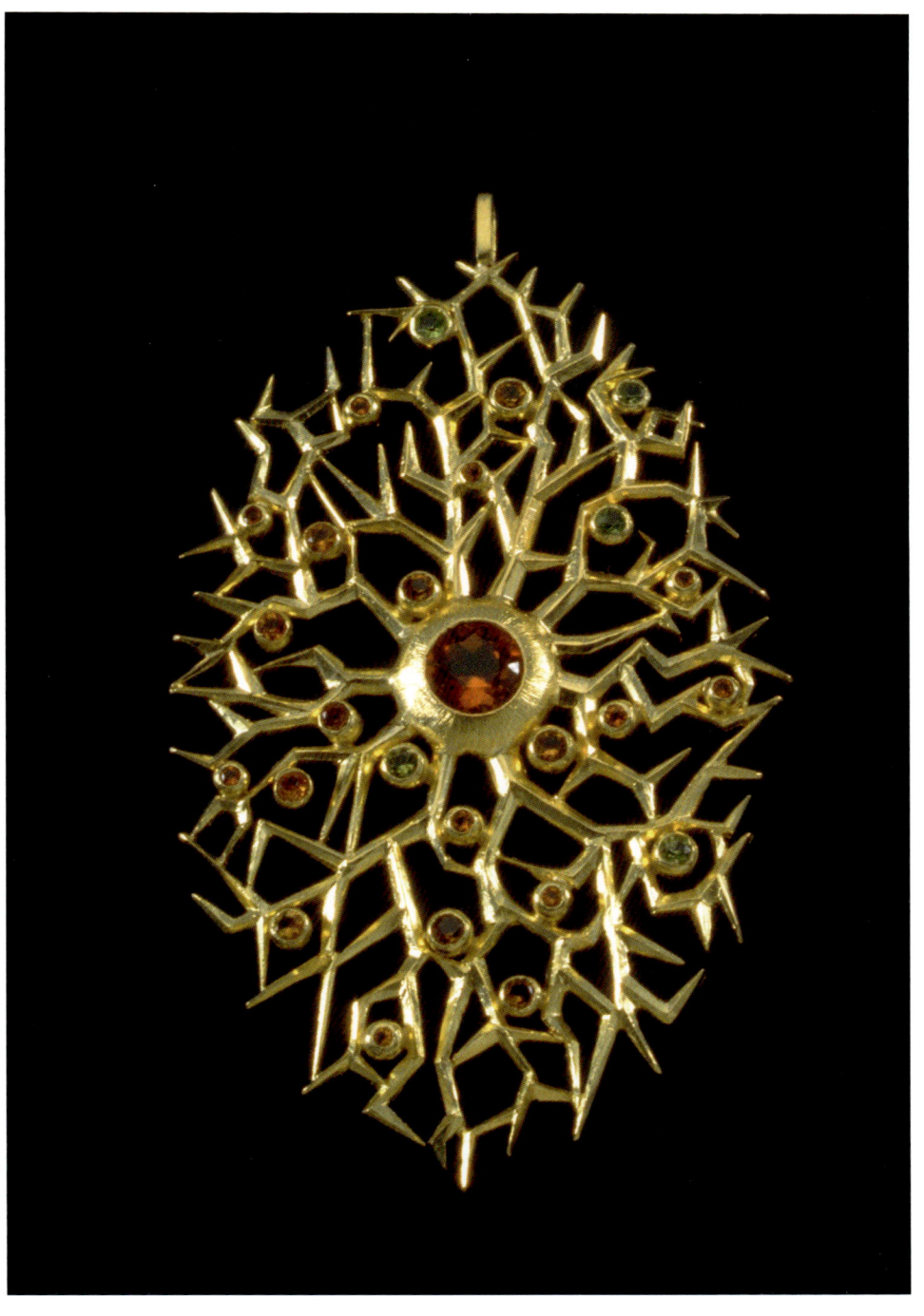

Ingeborg Bratman
1935-2015

Austrian-born Ingeborg Ruth Bratman arrived in England in 1938 with her family. As Jews, from Vienna and Budapest, they were fleeing from the Nazi rampage through Europe. Bratman's father set up a successful textile business in Huddersfield, West Yorkshire, called Jersey Craft.

In 1965, Bratman enrolled at Hornsey College of Art, and studied jewellery making under Gerda Flöckinger (see page 60), one of the greatest artist jewellers of her generation. Flöckinger experimented with fusing metals; her students have all been influenced by those experiments and many of them have used and worked with unusual metals themselves. Think Charlotte de Syllas and Jacqueline Mina.

After completing her course at Hornsey, Bratman continued her jewellery studies at the Sir John Cass College, also in London, until 1971, after which she set up independently. She sold her jewellery through Cameo Corner[1] and other retail outlets, and also undertook private commissions.

In the 1970s, Bratman started to work with tantalum, a notoriously difficult metal to work with and a metal nowadays more commonly used in industry than jewellery. The great advantage of using tantalum for wedding rings is that the metal is virtually scratch proof and is also hypoallergenic; the disadvantage is that the ring cannot be re-sized. Tantalum was discovered by the Swedish scientist Anders Gustaf Ekeberg in 1802. My own ancestor, William Hyde Wollaston PRS FRS, the famous chemist, experimented with columbium and tantalum in 1809 and concluded that the two oxides, despite their difference in measured density, were identical. The name tantalum, therefore, was kept and the previous name, columbium, was dropped. His papers on the subject are in the Royal Society.

Examples of Bratman's work with tantalum are in the V&A and the Science Museum, both in London.

---

1. Situated at 26 Museum Street in Bloomsbury, where it had been trading since 1938, Cameo Corner was *the* place to buy jewellery in London in the 1960s and 1970s. Many of the jewellery designers featured in this book exhibited there, including Bratman, Scott and Packard. The shop finally closed in 1978.

18ct white gold ring pavé-set with an oval-shaped light-green jade cabochon, maker's mark IRB, Ingeborg Bratman, 1975

Jocelyn Burton
1946-2020

A talented silversmith and jeweller, Sara Jocelyn Margarita Burton was made a Freeman of The Worshipful Company of Goldsmiths in 1974. She became something of a pioneer for women in her trade in 1966 when she applied to study silversmithing at the Sir John Cass College, London. She was accepted on to the course, but only part time, and so she changed to the college's full-time jewellery course by day, studying silversmithing in the evening.

Jocelyn Burton was an early winner (1968) of a De Beers Diamonds International Award with her gold necklace inset with diamonds, funded by her father, and a winner again in 1997 with a diamond necklace. After her studies, she worked for a master goldsmith in Hatton Garden for three years, but by the early 1970s she had opened her own studio, off Red Lion Street in Holborn, where she took commissions from the Livery companies and the Inns of Court who were her neighbours. She also travelled extensively in the Middle East (in particular in Saudi Arabia and Kuwait), Canada, India and, latterly, China.

For the Jerwood Foundation (founded by Alan Grieve CBE for John Jerwood MC in 1977), Burton designed the Jerwood Necklace in 1998, a £250,000 necklace made in gold with Pacific pearls,[1] black onyx, diamonds and a blue-star sapphire. Today, the necklace is housed in the Fitzwilliam Museum, Cambridge. She also designed the first piece of platinum to be hallmarked, in celebration of the Hallmarking Act of 1973.

In 2003, Burton became the first and (thus far) only woman to receive the Prince Philip Medal, the top engineering award from the City and Guilds of London Institute. It led to an article in the *Guardian* newspaper[2] asking why it had taken four decades for a woman to win this coveted top prize. She had previously made a pair of mustard pots, with octopus-shaped finials, for Prince Philip in 1997/8, which he subsequently presented to The Fishmonger's Company.

Fifteen pieces of Burton's tableware, made in sterling silver in the 1970s, came up at auction in the USA in 2021 and made interesting prices. They were originally commissioned by Philip Refson who was an American client and a friend of both Jocelyn Burton and Charles de Temple (see page 34).

Burton's work is in collections all over the world, including the V&A, London.

---

1. John Michael Jerwood MC (1918-1991) moved to Tokyo from London and established one of the largest pearl dealerships in the world, The Cultured Pearl Export Company.
2. Peter Kingston, "Better Late Than Never", *Guardian*, 29 July 2003.

18ct gold, diamond and Burmese ruby brooch, 1971

  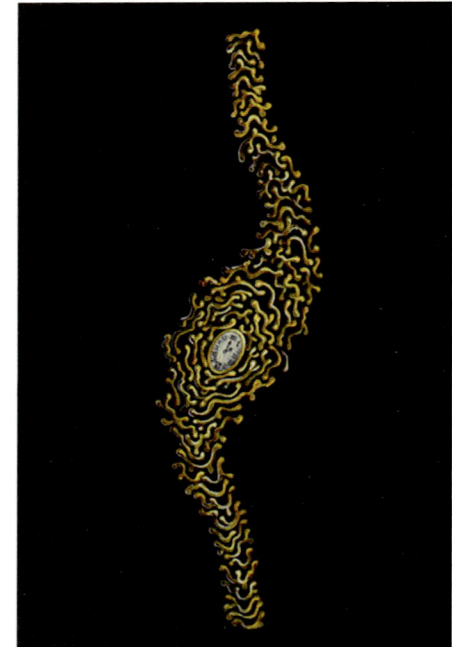

Sketches, left to right:
18ct gold necklace, granulated, with pearls and diamonds

18ct gold necklace, featuring articulated shapes of gold, with pearls, semi-precious stones and threads of white gold, echoing Burton's De Beers winning diamond necklace of 1967

18ct gold watch, designed for Watches of Switzerland, with 'molten' gold strap; a similar watch was made and sold for £885 in 1969

All three pieces were designed for Sydney Roger of Watches of Switzerland and Charles de Temple's new Bond Street shop, Galerie Jean Renet, 1969.

The company Jean Renet Ltd was incorporated on 27 February 1969. It was defunct by 1999. Both Burton and Charles de Temple were involved in the mysterious Galerie Jean Renet, a brand retailing both silver and jewellery through Watches of Switzerland in Old Bond Street, London. Burton is said to have stopped working for Galerie Jean Renet in 1973 after she was asked to make "an outrageous powder puff" in silver, in the form of a human penis.

"JOCELYN BURTON IS ONE OF LIFE'S ORIGINALS, AN EXPLOSIVE, OPINIONATED, BUBBLING BEING, ALL OF WHICH IS AMPLY REFLECTED IN HER WORK. EVERYTHING IS VERY EXACT AND TECHNICALLY PERFECT."

Sir Roy Strong

Preparatory sketches for the Jerwood Necklace, with Pacific pearls, black onyx, diamonds and a blue-star sapphire, 1998

Charles de Temple
1929-unknown

Charles de Temple, who could be described as the wild card in this pack, first appeared in London in about 1957, arriving from the USA. Proof that he was, indeed, working in the UK at this time was recently evidenced when one of his famous necklaces featuring pearls wrapped in 18ct gold came up at auction. The piece was British hallmarked 1957.[1] De Temple went on to produce some beautiful jewellery from his UK workshop during the 1960s and 1970s.

One of the secrets of de Temple's success was his response to the growing need to move away from traditional design in jewellery. Finding a public eager for modernity, he swiftly became known for his pioneering designs, which took on an organic and unique personality to reflect the individual wearer.

De Temple opened a shop at 52 Jermyn Street, London, where, according to Graham Hughes, he also lived, presumably in a flat above the shop. The entire building was owned by Philip Refson in the late 1970s, through to the early 1990s. Refson, a United States citizen, was a good friend and client of the silversmith, Jocelyn Burton (see page 28), as was Charles de Temple. In addition to selling his jewellery to private clients, de Temple kept some of Burton's silver work in his vaults and she exhibited and sold it through the Jermyn Street shop.

Charles de Temple also traded through the Watches of Switzerland showroom at 14 New Bond Street, London. The black boxes he had made for this purpose bore his gilt facsimile signature on the outside, while inside the wording on the silk lining read: "Designed Exclusively for Watches of Switzerland Ltd, 14 New Bond Street, W1".

One such design is the wonderfully sculptural ring pictured opposite. The virtually colourless stone is possibly a goshenite beryl from the town of Goshen in Hampshire County, Massachusetts. Massachusetts was well known to de Temple as it was where he set himself up as a jeweller before coming to England in the 1950s.

The goshenite ring is part of de Temple's "nervous jewels" series, so called for the prickly nature of the designs created using two-coloured gold wire. A necklace and a matching bracelet made c.1969-1975 are in the National Museums Scotland collection.[2]

De Temple seems to have disappeared from the London scene somewhere around 1992. His artistic legacy, however, lives on in the form of beautiful jewellery that still achieves high prices whenever it comes up at auction. There are also many pieces by de Temple in private collections all over the world. His work can be seen at Goldsmiths' Hall and the V&A, both in London, and in the collection of the National Museums Scotland.

---

1. Elmwood's, lot 108, 24 July 2019.
2. Refs K2016. 12. K2016. 13. On view: National Museums Collections Centre.

Above:
Ruby and diamond ring, 18ct yellow gold, brilliant-cut diamond accents, with a bombe panel pavé-set with similarly cut diamonds and circular-cut rubies, diamonds approx. 0.6oct total, maker's mark C de T, 1966

Left:
Two-colour 18ct gold and beryl-set dress ring, centred with a round-cut yellow-green beryl in four-claw mount, maker's mark CDet, 1969

Leo de Vroomen
b. 1941

Dutch goldsmith Leo de Vroomen came to Britain in 1965, having qualified as a Master Goldsmith in Switzerland a year earlier. Initially, he worked for a costume jewellery company in London where he met David Thomas (see page 146), the soon-to-be famous jeweller, who had a holiday job there whilst he was a student at the Central School of Art and Design. Through David, de Vroomen found a teaching job at the Central School, initially for one day per week, and then later for two days each week.

In his second year of teaching, de Vroomen met Ginnie, a first-year student who was studying life drawing under Ken Howard RA. She was to become de Vroomen's wife in 1970, and his design partner over the next 50 years.

De Vroomen and David Thomas worked together out of David's studio in Old Church Street, Chelsea, until 1968 when de Vroomen set up his own workshop in South West London. He revitalised the art of repoussé, a technique used to create flowing sculptural forms, and this was to become a feature of his work. In the same year (1968), de Vroomen took a showcase of his work to the USA.

The de Vroomen husband-and-wife team won a De Beers Diamonds International Award in 1974, and again in 1986. In 1977, the de Vroomens first showed their work at the Basel Fair, which they continued to do for the next 25 years.

The Worshipful Company of Goldsmiths gave an exhibition for Leo de Vroomen in 1991 at Goldsmiths' Hall, and again in 2017. Entitled Harmony in Colour and Form, this retrospective exhibition celebrated five decades of de Vroomen jewellery. De Vroomen also featured in the Goldsmiths' Company's exhibition of June 1997, British Master Goldsmiths. This exhibition featured 24 internationally known makers and designers of contemporary jewellery and silverware. A de Vroomen necklace was prominently displayed on the front cover of the flyer used to promote the exhibition.

In 2017, Leo and Ginnie produced their own beautifully illustrated hardback book, *de Vroomen*, showing their work over the last 50 years, which can be found in their elegant showroom in Elizabeth Street, London, which they opened in 2002.

Early work from the 1970s by this talented pair is hard to find. Pieces rarely come up at auction and are loved by their owners and handed down from one generation to the next. Nevertheless, collectors should persevere, because their work between 1970 and 1979 shows a wonderful, free-flowing form and an exceptional quality of craftsmanship.

De Vroomen jewellery can be found in the collection of The Worshipful Company of Goldsmiths at Goldsmiths' Hall, London.

18ct gold diamond ring, textured band with a row of collet-set brilliant-cut diamonds between two polished borders, 1979; 18ct gold diamond-set fancy link bracelet with collet-set diamonds, 1979; both with maker's mark LDV

Left:
Bangle, combining repoussé piercing and subtly applied wire work, made for Hooper Bolton, early 1970s

Right, above:
Brooch, combining repoussé and wire forms, 1970

Right, below:
Kunzite and diamond brooch, early 1970s

Citrine and diamond brooch, c.1970

18ct gold necklet featuring a hollow reversible pendant, made using repoussé technique, mid-1970s

Stuart Devlin CMG
1931-2018

Stuart Leslie Devlin, who was born in Australia, was an artist and metalworker specialising in gold and silver. He came to London in 1960, on a scholarship to study at the Royal College of Art, and then rose to prominence four years later, as the winner of a competition to design the first decimal coinage for Australia. In 1965, Devlin opened a small workshop where he devised new techniques to provide a variety of designs, often in limited editions, which ranged from Easter eggs and Christmas boxes to goblets and insignia.

In the late 1960s, Devlin started to make pieces of jewellery. In general, his jewellery work was quite sculptural, masculine, even. It concentrated more on the fine metal (as you would expect from a leading silver and goldsmith) and less on the stones, which were almost always semi-precious.

Before Devlin opened his own shop in Conduit Street, London (1979-1983), he was fortunate enough to work in partnership with the 6th Duke of Westminster to sell his jewellery through the Royal jewellers, Collingwood, who launched an exhibition called A Silversmith for Today at their own showrooms in Conduit Street in 1972. The exhibition catalogue had an excellent foreword by A. Kenneth Snowman, Chairman of Wartski.

In 1980, HM The Queen appointed Devlin a Companion of the Order of St Michael and St George (CMG) "for service to the art of design". In 1982, he was granted the Royal Warrant of Appointment as Goldsmith and Silversmith to Her Majesty The Queen. In the following year, The Worshipful Company of Goldsmiths offered Devlin a one-man retrospective exhibition at Goldsmiths' Hall. His pieces were loaned from all over the world and the queues to see his work went around the block and back again.

When HRH Princess Margaret's jewellery collection came up for auction at Christie's in June 2006, Devlin was one of seven UK-based independent jewellers or goldsmiths whose work was represented. The others were Andrew Grima, John Donald, Alan Gard, Michael Gosschalk, Leslie Durbin and Theo Fennell. The 18ct gold macle diamond crystal ring Devlin made for Princess Margaret was catalogued as lot 43, London hallmarked, and dated 1977; it was sold with Devlin's distinctive black leather ring box. The guide price was £2,000 to £3,000 but it sold for £30,000, testament to both the greatness of the man and the exceptional circumstances of the sale.

Writing the foreword to a Devlin monograph in 2018, just before Devlin died, HRH Prince Philip, Duke of Edinburgh, described him as "probably the most original and creative goldsmith and silversmith of his time, and one of the greats of all time."[1]

Examples of Devlin's silver and gold work can be found in the collection of The Worshipful Company of Goldsmiths and the V&A, both in London.

---

1. Carole Devlin and Victoria Kate Simkin, eds, *Stuart Devlin: Designer, Goldsmith, Silversmith* (Woodbridge; ACC Art Books, 2018), 9.

Amethyst and cultured pearl brooch and ring,
maker's mark SD, 1976

44

Diamond and lapis lazuli-set ring, 18ct white gold,
maker's mark SD, 1976

18ct gold brooch, maker's mark SD, 1979

46

White and yellow gold figured brooch, the figures layered around triangular diamonds, surrounding a large green tourmaline, c.1972. Much of Devlin's jewellery featured tiny human beings worked in precious metal as a design feature

Curling brooch, with yellow, white and red gold figures curling around a central ruby, supported by white diamonds, 1972

John Donald
b. 1928

John Alistair Donald is a gold and silversmith, a jeweller and a designer. He studied metalsmithing at the Royal College of Art from 1952 to 1955, under Professor Robert Goodden, and won a Travelling Scholarship to Italy in 1955. Later, Donald worked as a design consultant for the Hadley spectacle frame company for almost a decade, during which time he was also commissioned by The Worshipful Company of Goldsmiths to make badges for the Wardens, in 1959. He set up his own workshop in Bayswater, London, in 1960, and won a De Beers award for jewellery three years later.

In 1961, Donald took part in the International Exhibition of Modern Jewellery 1890-1961 in London. He exhibited three brooches and a badge (lent by the Mayor of Lincoln), made between 1958 and 1961.[1]

In 1964, the Earl of Snowdon introduced HRH Princess Margaret and HM Queen Elizabeth The Queen Mother to John Donald, and they became patrons of his work. When the dispersal sale of the Princess's jewellery by Christie's took place in June 2006, Donald was one of the seven British designers whose work was represented. HRH had 16 pieces of his jewellery in her collection, which was way more than any other designer, and included the pieces using Pierre Gilson's synthetic emeralds.[2] The prices fetched by Donald's work were phenomenal; for instance, £142,400 for a diamond ring in its original brown suede "John Donald" box. However, when it came to the pieces set with the synthetic emeralds the prices were lower, reflecting that, even in 2006, the public remained suspicious of anything that was not, as they saw it, the genuine article.

In 1959, Donald became a Freeman of The Worshipful Company of Goldsmiths and was made a Liveryman in 1970. In 1968, he opened his gallery and workshop at 120 Cheapside, London, which ran successfully for more than 35 years, until the site was claimed for redevelopment at the end of January 2005.

The "cube", originally designed in 1963, was a recurring theme in Donald's work. In the pendant/brooch, made in 1963, that The Worshipful Company of Goldsmiths have in their collection, he used diamonds, and the striated cubes are made in 18ct yellow gold. In the brooch and matching earrings (see pages 54 and 55), the striated cubes are made entirely of 18ct yellow gold with no diamonds. Donald made this demi-parure in 1968, the last year in which the price of gold was "pegged" at $35 per ounce and the year that the London Gold Pool subsequently collapsed (see introduction, page 12). This matching set would have cost considerably more to make the following year, when gold was already $40 per ounce and rising fast.

Donald has always worked for private commissions but some of his work features in public collections, including The Worshipful Company of Goldsmiths, London, the National Museum of Scotland, Edinburgh, and the V&A, London.

---

1. The badge was illustrated in the catalogue as plate 86.
2. Pierre Gilson; the French physicist invented his process for "growing" emeralds at Campagne-lez-Wardrecques in 1965.

18ct yellow gold ring with red spinel mineral to the centre, maker's mark JAD, 1967

50

18ct yellow gold abstract bracelet, with textured gold cubes, and set with square sapphires and circular-cut diamonds, maker's mark JAD, 1968

Left:
18ct gold brooch with pearls and coral, maker's mark JAD, 1971

Right:
John Donald advert from *The Field* magazine, November 1999 (p. 134)

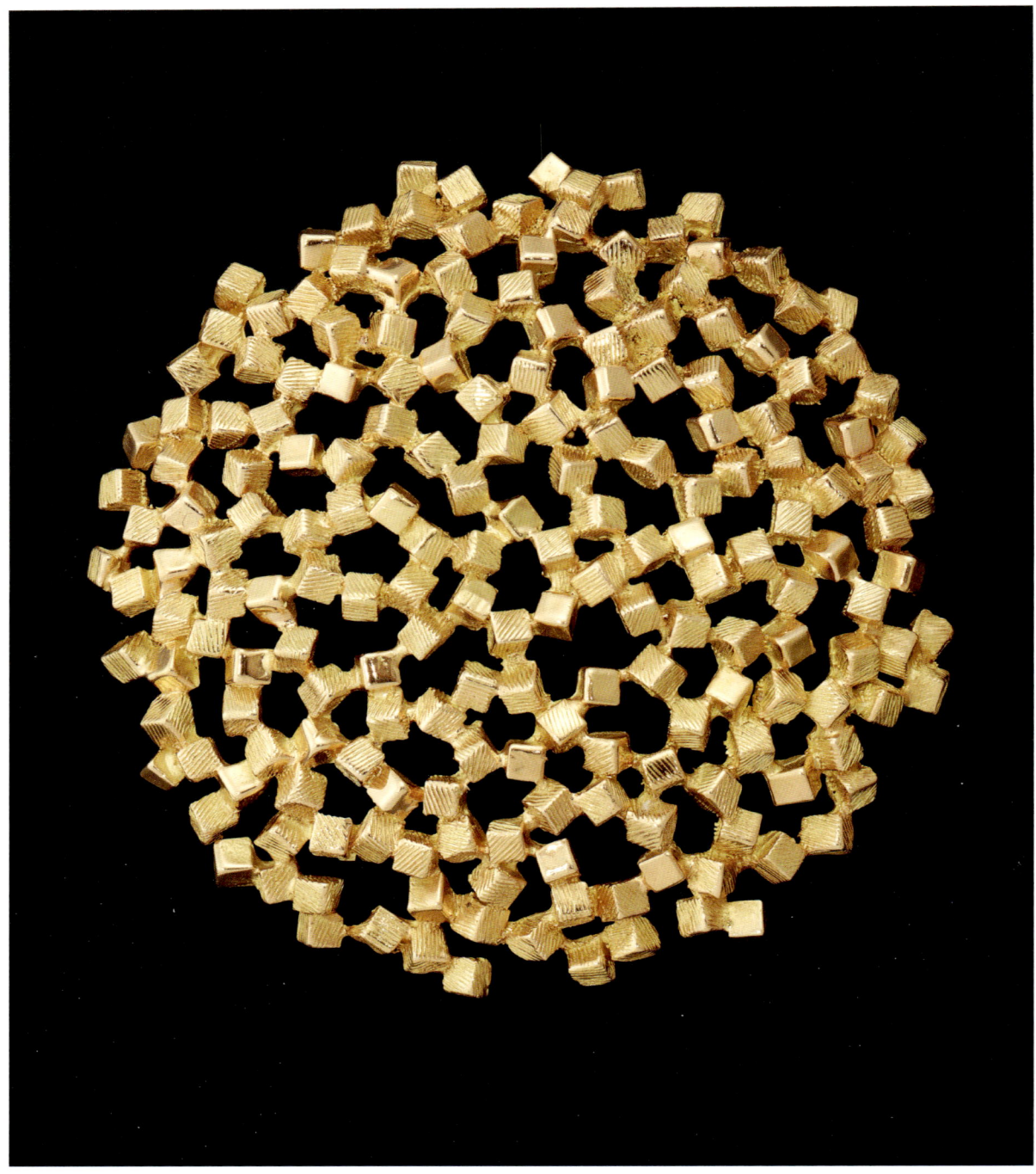

Brooch and earrings in 18ct striated gold cubes,
maker's mark JAD, 1968

Rod Edwards
1921-1985

Rod Leslie Edwards was born in Sydney, Australia. He was apprenticed to the firm Angus & Coote, where he worked under the direction of Lionel "Nugget" Paton, probably Australia's finest jeweller.

Edwards studied jewellery and design at Sydney Art School and exhibited his work as both a sculptor and maker of jewellery between 1940 and 1950. In 1948, he was appointed head lecturer of jewellery at Sydney Art School. He left Australia in 1951, settled in England, and worked for leading firms such as Corocraft[1] (1954-1960), before setting up his own workshop in London in 1960.

In 1961, Edwards lent a pendant made in silver set with turquoise on one side and garnet on the other to the International Exhibition of Modern Jewellery 1890-1961.[2] Sadly, there is no extant illustration, so we cannot tell what the pendant looked like. However, a number of surviving pendant and ring illustrations, including one of an 18ct gold ring with a cat's eye-green sapphire, featured in Edwards' extremely technical book on jewellery making in 1977, offering an insight into his style.[3] *The Technique of Jewellery* featured a large number of illustrations by Edwards' wife, Virginia Smith.

In the same year that his book was published, Edwards took part in a two-man exhibition at the famous Electrum Gallery with David Hensel where, according to Hensel, "we sold everything and got it all started".[4] Hensel may have been at the start of a long association with the legendary Barbara Cartlidge and the Electrum Gallery, but Edwards never exhibited there again, although the reasons for this are not clear.

Edwards' work, which tends to be highly individualistic and sculptural, has been sold in London at Fortnum & Mason, The Craft Gallery and The Craft Centre, and by David Hall in Stratford-upon-Avon and John Kelly in Bristol (see opposite). His commissions have included trophies for the Olympic Games in 1968 and 1972, and a gold sphere and medallion, which were commissioned by The Worshipful Company of Goldsmiths to commemorate the opening of the Sydney Opera House in 1973.

Edwards lectured at the Camden Institute in London and worked on private commissions but suffered periods of debilitating depression and anguished over detail, which affected his career intermittently. Indeed, Tom Scott (see page 142) remembers being called upon at short notice to give one of Edwards' lectures for him.

Edwards' work is represented in the collections of The Worshipful Company of Goldsmiths and the V&A in London; the Powerhouse Museum, Sydney; and the National Museum of Scotland, Edinburgh.

---

1. Part of the Coro Company making costume jewellery. They went out of business in 1979.
2. Item no. 237 in the International Exhibition of Modern Jewellery 1890-1961 catalogue.
3. Rod Edwards, *The Technique of Jewellery* (London: B.T. Batsford, 1977), 121.
4. Beatriz Chadour-Sampson and Janice Hosegood, *Barbara Cartlidge and Electrum Gallery: A Passion for Jewellery* (Stuttgart: Arnoldsche Art, 2016), 150.

Silver and lapis lazuli brooch, the oval stone raised
on a colonnade, stamped RLE for Rod Edwards, 1963

Silver pendant brooch with central green tourmaline cabochon, maker's mark RLE, stamped Rod Edwards, 1965

Gerda Flöckinger CBE
b. 1927

Born in 1927 in Innsbruck, Austria, Gerda Flöckinger came to England in 1938. She studied fine art at Saint Martins School of Art in London, and from 1952 to 1956 jewellery techniques and enamelling at the Central School of Arts and Crafts. In 1956, she set up to become an independent designer jeweller, which was an unusual move for that time

In her early work, Flöckinger experimented with enamels and rough gems. From the early 1960s, she came to rely more on flame and fusion techniques, arriving at an intensely original and personal style incorporating texture and fluidity. Movement, which is very evident in her work, is achieved by using fine rods of half-melted spiral threads.

From 1962 to 1968, Flöckinger established an experimental course in jewellery at Hornsey College of Art for artist jewellers whose goals diverged from the traditional. She taught many of the emerging non-conformist talents, including Charlotte de Syllas and Ingeborg Bratman (see page 26).

Flöckinger was the first living female designer to have an exhibition at the V&A Museum, in 1971, and her work was shown there again in 1986. She was also the first designer to be commissioned by the V&A to produce a piece of jewellery for their permanent collection of contemporary art, illustrating her importance as a pioneer in the revival of jewellery designing and making in the UK.

In 1991, Flöckinger was recognised by HM The Queen for her contribution to the arts and awarded a CBE. She was made a Freeman of The Worshipful Company of Goldsmiths in 1998, and in 2006 she was made an Honorary Fellow of the University of the Arts, London.

The necklace shown opposite, made of silver, 18ct gold, grey cultured baroque pearls, small white pearls and diamonds, with a citrine clasp, was created in 1977 and exhibited at 'Schmuckobjekte' at Galerie Atrium, Basel, Switzerland, in 1978. It is a perfect showcase of Flöckinger's considerable vocabulary of fusion techniques, many of which she had invented and developed during the 1960s. Flöckinger used fusion to create an elaborate, enriched surface and is one of the few artists to have fused gold to silver and vice versa. She made several versions of these necklaces.

Flöckinger's work is represented in many private collections. Public collections include The Worshipful Company of Goldsmiths; the National Museum of Scotland, Edinburgh; the Craft Council; and the Museum of Fine Arts, Boston, USA. Several of Flöckinger's early pieces can be seen in the William and Judith Bollinger Gallery at the V&A, London.

Above and following page:
18ct gold necklace, with sliver, pearls and diamonds, with citrine clasp, maker's mark GF, 1977 (detail overleaf). Exhibited at 'Schmuckobjekte' at Galerie Atrium, Basel, Switzerland in 1978

62

"I WORK ON EVOCATION. I TRY TO EVOKE CERTAIN EMOTIONS, CERTAIN FEELINGS. I'M LOOKING FOR A SENSE OF EXCITEMENT OR ZING. THIS IS VERY DIFFICULT TO ACHIEVE AND I ALWAYS FEEL WHILE I'M WORKING ON A PIECE THAT IT DIES MANY TIMES. BUT WITH LUCK, WHEN IT'S ALL FINISHED AND ALL THE ELEMENTS ARE THERE AND ALL THE COLOURS ARE FINALLY PUT IN, IT WILL HAVE ZING."

Gerda Flöckinger

Elizabeth Gage MBE
b. 1937

Elizabeth Gage is an award-winning British jewellery designer and a trained master goldsmith who has been creating collectable jewellery for more than 50 years. Her style is uniquely her own and does not follow a fashion line; she is not defined by the Sixties and Seventies' passion for raw stones, for example. Rather, her style at that time was influenced by her love of the Plantagenet period in history (1154-1485) and the Knights Templar.

Gage enrolled in the silver department at the Sir John Cass College in 1964, before moving to the jewellery department when it opened under Frank Oliver. Gage does not give us a date for this move, but she does say in her book, *The Unconventional Gage* (2003), that at the time gold cost $35 per ounce. This means that it must have been some time before March 1968, after which gold was no longer "pegged" at $35 an ounce (see Introduction for more on gold pegging).

Gage's first commission was for Cartier in New York. Her designs appeared in their 1968 catalogue and were so successful they had to be reordered. She works in 18 and 22ct gold and still designs every piece that bears her name.

In 1972, Gage won a coveted De Beers Diamonds International Award for her Agincourt ring. The Diamonds International Awards, sponsored by De Beers, originated in 1953. The last edition of these biennial competitions took place in 2000. The awards were considered to be the "Oscars" of the jewellery industry. In 1989, Gage won The Queen's Award for Export Achievement, and the award ceremony was held at Claridge's, along with a retrospective exhibition of her work.

Her work is represented in the permanent collection of jewellery at the V&A Museum, London, by whom Gage was commissioned to design and produce a piece for inclusion in an exhibition of tiaras in 2002. The V&A also held an Elizabeth Gage retrospective exhibition, by invitation, in 1996. Gage's maternal line is American and she has held one-woman shows in Palm Beach, Chicago, San Francisco, New York, Houston, Dallas and Los Angeles each year since the early 1970s, so it is not surprising that her following includes a great number of American collectors. She moved her showroom from Albemarle Street, London, where she had been for 20 years, to her present address at 5 West Halkin Street in 2012. She was awarded an MBE in 2017.

Above:
18ct gold Leo Zodiac Templar band ring, c.1964

Left:
18ct gold Agincourt band, set alternately with peridots and amethysts, 1967

Left:
18ct gold Charlemagne ring set with nineteenth-century blue glass intaglio of Janus, c.1965

Right:
18ct gold Kiss pin set with silver-grey pearls in wire cones, 1967; and matching 18ct gold African Queen earrings, c.1968

Alan Gard
b. 1935

Alan Martin Gard is a goldsmith and a jeweller. He was born in London and apprenticed for seven years under the Bond Street jewellers, Crombies. He also worked for Andrew Grima, at the HJ Company workshop, in 1964. He did not exhibit at the 1961 International Exhibition of Modern Jewellery 1890-1961, but he is a seriously important designer and a tremendous character.

I once took a signed pendant of his, which I had bought in the US, to Gard's workshop to see if he could date it. He could not but, ever helpful, suggested that I take it round to the Assay Office to see if they could. With hindsight, I realise that he probably wanted to get rid of me because he had another client to see. Instead of taking me there himself, he popped his head round the workshop door and shouted, "Maud, can you take this lady to the Assay Office?" Maud shouted back, "No, I can't!" "Why not?" asked Gard. "Because I don't want to," she yelled, with typical Cockney bluntness. In the end she did take me, and she was charming!

Gard, also a Cockney, born and bred around the corner from the workshop he has had for the past 40 years, knows every inch of Hatton Garden. A photo of Harry Oppenheimer, the diamond king and ex-chairman of De Beers, is stuck on his wall. Oppenheimer's driver was a good friend of Gard's, so Gard met the great man from time to time during his frequent trips from South Africa to his headquarters at 17 Charterhouse Street, London.

Shortly after the Maud incident, I was fortunate enough to acquire an early brooch by Gard at a provincial auction. It is signed and dated 1966. I was so thrilled with my purchase that I pinned it to my jacket lapel and knocked on Gard's door. As he opened the door he cried, "My brooch!" which was quite amazing because it was more than 50 years since he had last seen it. Absolutely delighted, he went to a cupboard, pulled out an old ledger book and said, "Look, this brooch is number 28 in my ledger book, the year I started out on my own after my apprenticeship with Andrew Grima."

Alan Gard was one of the seven British designers whose work was included in the sale of Princess Margaret's jewellery, at Christie's in 2006. The brooch that he made for the Princess was a diamond-set cluster of 18ct gold lily pads. London hallmarked and dated 1967, it sold for £10,200.

Green dioptase crystal brooch within a textured openwork 18ct gold surround, accented by brilliant-cut diamonds, maker's mark AMG, 1972

Left:
18ct yellow gold, diamond and turquoise flower brooch, maker's mark AMG, 1966

Right:
18ct yellow gold and amethyst ring with diamonds, maker's mark, AMG, 1968

Left:
18ct two-colour gold and diamond necklace, comprising overlapping bark-textured panels with claw-set brilliant-cut diamonds, maker's mark AMG, 1974

Right:
18ct gold-set tourmaline brooch with six diamonds, maker's mark AMG, 1968

Michael Gosschalk
1923-2010

Michael Gosschalk's company, Michael Gosschalk Ltd, lent a rough gold and diamond flower brooch, signed by Geoffrey Turk[1] and dated 1961, to the International Exhibition of Modern Jewellery 1890-1961 (plate 92; catalogue no. 785). He also loaned two other pieces to the exhibition (catalogue nos. 425 and 426). The brooch was made by the HJ Company, whose managing director was Andrew Grima (see page 78).

Before opening his jewellery shop at 20 Motcomb Street, London, in 1957, Gosschalk had been working as a very successful stone merchant for seven years. This fact was not lost on the eccentric Dame Edith Sitwell,[2] who became one of Gosschalk's clients towards the end of her life. He supplied her with some of the enormous stone rings for which she became very well known, sometimes wearing two large rocks on one finger.

After Dame Edith died, her family presented three of her rings bearing Michael Gosschalk's stamp to the V&A Museum, London, where they are currently displayed at the recently refurbished William and Judith Bollinger Gallery.

I first met Andrew Grima through Michael Gosschalk and his French wife, Jenny Fischer, in 1959. Jenny was a society hat maker with a little shop at 16 Motcomb Street, and I was her hat model – a very happy association for us both. Jenny made hats for a number of the guests at Princess Margaret's wedding in 1960, including creations for the Hon. Iris Peake MVO (Princess Margaret's lady-in-waiting) and the young Duchess of Fife. Michael's and Jenny's shops were a few doors apart, on the same side of the road, and the family lived at number 16, above Jenny's hat shop.

Andrew Grima, having no retail outlet himself at that time, sold his jewellery exclusively through Michael Gosschalk's shop until 1962. Indeed, Gosschalk was a hugely influential figure in the London jewellery world between 1957 and 1965, largely because, through his jewellery, he brought fun and glamour back into everyday life in a then unfashionable part of London, which was still gripped by wartime austerity and red tape.

Everybody wanted to be part of the Gosschalk set, and both husband and wife had a great number of influential clients. These clients were younger than the conservative Bond Street buyers and they were throwing off the shackles that bound them to a West End formality. This is backed up by Elizabeth Benn, a journalist on the *Daily Telegraph and Morning Post*, who wrote an article, "A Change from Bond Street Glitter", about the International Exhibition of

---

1. Geoffrey Turk (1928-2016): an important designer who worked with Andrew Grima for the HJ Company for 35 years.
2. Dame Edith Sitwell (1887-1964): poet and author who indulged a passion for eye-catching jewellery, particularly large rings.
3. Elizabeth Benn, "A Change from Bond Street Glitter", *Daily Telegraph and Morning Post*, Thursday 26 October 1961.
4. *London Gazette*, 3 December 1965.

Top:
Petal brooch made of topaz with a diamond and topaz centre

Bottom:
Amethyst petal brooch with a diamond centre

Modern Jewellery 1890-1961 at Goldsmiths' Hall, in which she said that "Kutchinsky and Michael Gosschalk probably make the nearest thing we have to modern jewellery in this country."[3] The Kutchinsky and Gosschalk jewellery houses were both based in Knightsbridge and not the West End. Both houses used precious and semi-precious stones, and their designs were pretty rather than sculptural, which shows where Benn's taste in jewellery lay at the time.

The Gosschalks were a most attractive couple who seemed to be very much at the top of their game in the early 1960s, so it came as a shock when Michael's business closed in November 1965.[4] It followed a major heist in the previous August, when a four-man gang wearing stocking masks and armed with pickaxes stole £50,000 from the shop, traumatising the sales staff and a woman customer who were made to lie on the floor. The raid also made an overnight hero of a nine-year-old boy who, passing by in a chauffeur-driven car, and seeing the gang attempt to make their escape, instructed the chauffeur to abandon the idea of taking him to school and to give chase instead, which, accompanied by the police, they did!

After Michael and Jenny left London to live in Monaco, Michael continued to make jewellery for his clients from his shop in Monte Carlo. Just occasionally, a beautiful example of his work from this period comes up at auction, such as the pink sapphire flower brooch which graced the catalogue cover at Bonhams in 2019 (see page 77). It bears French export marks and a London import stamp for 1970.

Michael Gosschalk had rather disappeared from the London jewellery scene by the time his coral and diamond earrings (lot 22) came up for auction at Christie's in 2006, in a sale featuring jewellery from the collection of HRH Princess Margaret. The earrings, made in 1960, the year that Princess Margaret married Antony Armstrong-Jones, were guided in the catalogue at £500 to £700 but achieved an astonishing £10,000. Her Royal Highness had been wise enough to keep them in Gosschalk's original grey suede box, which may have added to the rarity value. Gosschalk was one of only seven independent designers whose jewellery featured in the collection of the Princess.

Sketch of a diamond brooch (above) in the shape of a rose, created in the 1960s, along with the photograph (left) of the finished item, showing the process from concept to brooch, c.1960

Brooch in 18ct gold, pink sapphire and diamonds, maker's mark MG, 1970

Andrew Grima
1921-2007

Often no more than a slice of agate set with a small diamond and a thin ribbon of gold drizzled over one corner, Andrew Peter Grima's brooches and rings were – and still are – immeasurably stylish and wearable.

Grima trained as an engineer and served with the Royal Engineers in Burma during the Second World War. In 1947, he married Hélène Haller, whose stepfather, Franz Haller, had started a tiny jewellery manufacturing business in London called HJ Company. Grima worked with Franz Haller until the latter's death in 1951 and then took over the business as managing director.

This innovative jewellery designer won many awards, including 13 De Beers Diamonds International Awards, the Duke of Edinburgh's Prize for Elegant Design, and the Queen's Award for Export Achievement 1966. He opened his famous shop, designed by his architect brothers Godfrey and George, and Ove Arup, at 80 Jermyn Street, London, in 1966. Elected a Liveryman of The Worshipful Company of Goldsmiths in 1968, he received a Royal Warrant two years later.

Andrew Grima then set about marketing his jewellery designs all over the world. Sometimes, he travelled as a team with Graham Hughes, backed by The Worshipful Company of Goldsmiths; and sometimes with Geoffrey Turk, from his own HJ Company team.

He opened Grima shops in New York City, Zurich, Tokyo and Sydney, and hosted a series of innovative exhibitions, including the famous About Time exhibition, which was held at Goldsmiths' Hall and opened by HRH Anne, Princess Royal, on 4 May 1970. This was a collection of 86 pieces, 55 of them watches designed and made in collaboration with the Omega Watch Company, Switzerland.

Many of his themed exhibitions were hosted at 80 Jermyn Street and included Opals and Pearls (1970), Rock Revival (1971), Super Shells (1972), Sticks and Stones (1973) and A Tale of Tahiti (1974).

The swinging pearl ring in an open niche, like a bell tower, is a design that Grima favoured. He called these the "campanile" rings, made for the Opals and Pearls exhibition in December 1970, and he created several, slightly different versions.[1] A Grima swinging pearl ring from the 1970 exhibition turned up recently; it had been miscatalogued as a "1989 swinging pearl ring in white gold, stamped Grima and London hallmarked" (see page 85). The date was 1970 (the date letter P being similar but subtly different to the P used for 1989). The clue lay in the HJ Company workshop stamp, which was not mentioned at all in the catalogue description, and which had been phased out altogether by 1973 (and certainly by 1989) in favour of the workshop stamp, AG Ltd. Grima's jewellery was revolutionary in the 1960s – and still is. His

---

1. One of Grima's campanile rings, featuring three swinging pearls set in 18ct gold, is illustrated in Johann Willsberger's book on six leading jewellers (6 Meister Juweliere, Zeit, 1971), in the section devoted to Grima.

use of the brutalist style in many of his designs (it was, after all, the age of Sir Basil Spence and his angular concrete buildings) was wonderfully effective in his brooches and pendants, but lethal in his rings, which could tear a jacket lining as you put your arm through the sleeve if you didn't take care. Unlike George Weil (see page 152), Grima made no concession to tame the sharp points of the ring with little caps of gold.

Carved rubies were most famously used in a Grima brooch now in the personal collection of HM The Queen. In the catalogue for his retrospective exhibition, held at Goldsmiths' Hall in 1991, Grima says that the brooch was made in 1965, using rubies from an old Indian ornament, which means that the rubies had already been carved by lapidaries (the Indians had embraced the practice of carving jewels since early times) and were therefore vintage.

In 2015, Bonhams sold a 2.97ct greyish-blue diamond ring by Andrew Grima for £1,482,500, a world record for any piece of Grima sold at auction. The ring was London hallmarked and dated 1971.

Examples of Grima's work can be found in the V&A, London, and in the permanent collection of The Worshipful Company of Goldsmiths at Goldsmiths' Hall, London, where Grima became a Freeman and a Liveryman.

18ct yellow gold brooch set with 10 sapphires, five diamonds and three cultured pearls, maker's mark HJCo, 1964

Above left:
18ct gold lapis lazuli and diamond ring, rectangular lapis lazuli accented by a row of brilliant-cut diamonds to either side with a geometric textured band, maker's mark HJCo, 1969

Above:
18ct yellow gold, diamond and sapphire brooch, maker's mark HJCo, 1962

Left:
18ct yellow gold and diamond ring, maker's mark HJCo, 1964

18ct yellow gold, 1.5ct diamond and emerald brooch pendant with additional detachable carved drop, maker's mark HJCo, 1964

18ct gold ring with 14 round diamonds, maker's mark HJCo, Duke of Edinburgh's Prize, 1966

"I SAW GOLD IN ITS 'RAW' STATE WITH STONES GROWING FROM ITS CENTRE WITHOUT CLAWS AND WITHOUT FUSS."

Andrew Grima

18ct yellow gold abstract brooch, signed GRIMA, 1968

18ct white gold suspended pearl drop ring, maker's mark HJCo, signed GRIMA, 1970

Far left:
18ct yellow gold and fluorite brooch with four diamonds, maker's mark HJCo & Grima, 1967

Above:
18ct gold and citrine pendant brooch, earrings and ring suite with diamonds, maker's mark AGLtd, signed GRIMA, 1973

Left:
18ct gold textured wire diamond-set brooch, maker's mark HJCo, 1965

88

Left:
18ct gold, fire opal and diamond brooch pendant, maker's mark HJCo, signed GRIMA, 1964

Right:
18ct gold and diamond brooch in the form of a shaped rectangular panel with eye aperture, maker's mark AGLtd, signed GRIMA, 1976

Left:
18ct 'molten' yellow gold oval cabochon moonstone pendant with two brilliant-cut diamonds, maker's mark AGLtd, signed GRIMA, 1976

Right:
18ct yellow gold double-pin brooch pendant, mounted with 10 carved cabochon emeralds and nine brilliant-cut diamonds, signed HJCo, 1968

18ct yellow gold textured wire, druzy agate, emerald, diamond and ruby brooch pendant, maker's mark HJCo, 1965

18ct gold citrine brooch pendant, maker's mark
AGLtd, signed GRIMA, 1977, featured in the Grima
1991 Retrospective exhibition

93

A triangular geode pendant, triangular slice of
white chalcedony mounted within a gold frame with
textured corners, maker's mark AGLtd, 1977

Alfred Gruber / Jacqueline Stieger
1931-1972 / b. 1936

Alfred Gruber was born at Steuerberg in Austria. In 1948, he studied at the Linz Art School under the guidance of the Austrian sculptor, Walter Ritter. On completion of his studies, Gruber travelled to Italy, Germany, Belgium, Holland and England, where he visited the sculpture studio of Henry Moore.

In 1953, he moved to Switzerland and was initially employed as a monumental mason before securing a position as a stone carver with Swiss sculptor, Albert Schilling, at Arlesheim, near Basel.

Gruber met Jacqueline Stieger in 1962, by which time he had left Schilling's employment and established his own workshop with a foundry at Laufen. The earliest reference to him exhibiting jewellery is in 1969, when he contributed to the Schmuck Moderner Meister exhibition at the Galerie D'Art Modern, in Basel. Fellow contributors included Hans Arp, Georges Braque and Alexander Calder.

Gruber and Stieger married in 1966 and spent the next few years together in Switzerland. In 1969 they moved to East Yorkshire, England, where they bought an old farm building in Welton, which they converted into a home with a workshop and a foundry.

Sadly, Gruber died of lung cancer in February 1972; he was just 41 years old. His work is represented by two brooches in the permanent collection of The Worshipful Company of Goldsmiths, London, and by the panel brooch pictured on page 96, which is in our collection.

Jacqueline Stieger studied painting at Edinburgh College of Art from 1953 to 1959. She now works as a sculptor, jeweller and medallist. Most of her pieces are cast in gold, silver or bronze, using the lost-wax technique. Her work varies from large pieces of sculpture to small and intricate items of jewellery, and ranges from public commissions, work for universities and churches, to private commissions for individual clients.

Stieger does most of her own casting, a part of the making process which fascinates her, and the continuing path of creating forms with drawing, modelling and materials, which fit their context, is the challenge that forms the basis of her work.

Jacqueline Stieger was awarded the Freedom of The Worshipful Company of Goldsmiths in 1985 and, later, the Freedom of the City of London. She became a Fellow of the Royal Society of Arts in 1986.

Stieger has kept Gruber's maker's mark, AGS, registered in Sheffield, as her own. Examples of her jewellery and her medal work are in the permanent collections at Goldsmiths' Hall and the British Museum, London.

Far left:
Alfred Gruber in his studio at Laufen

Above:
Two rings: 18ct gold and 18ct gold with agate, c.1969

Left:
Bracelet in 18ct gold, c.1970

Left:
18ct gold brooch pendant designed as a segmented textured panel set with oval and semicircular opal cabochons, maker's mark AGS, 1970

Right:
Brooch in 18ct gold with moonstone, c.1970

Above left:
Brooch in 18ct gold with moonstones, c.1970

Above:
Jacqueline Stieger brooch in 18ct gold with orange moonstone, created using asphalt which was heated to a drop-in consistency where the various drops and dribbles are then manipulated to create abstract forms, 1973

Left:
Pendant brooch in silver with chrysoprase, c.1970

Right:
Pendant brooch in 18ct gold with turquoise and diamonds, 1970

Roger King
b. 1936

There are several talented jewellery designers whose early promise was extinguished by death, disease, drink or despair but only one whose exceptional talent was diverted, by the age of 25, into a completely different arena. The designer is Roger King, son of Roy King (see page 106), founder of a multi-million-pound business.

Roger Milner King studied (mostly part-time) at the Central School of Arts and Crafts in London, from 1953 to 1957. At the same time, he and his lifelong friend, Frank Lambert (also a jewellery designer), did their apprenticeship with King's father's company, Roy C. King Ltd.

In 1961, King swept the board in the De Beers Open Competition for Modern British Jewellery, winning two important first prizes and one second prize for his jewellery designs. Such was his triumph that he was featured as Man of the Month in the *Goldsmith's Journal*, where he was described as "a 25-year-old director of Roy C King Ltd, Watford fine jewellery manufacturers and director of two other companies".[1] The writing was on the wall, because the article pointed to his strong entrepreneurial streak, which was to show itself in the following years.

In 1962, King won the Jewel of the Year competition. His design – a brooch of diamonds and gold – was entered by Collingwood and displayed by Christie's on the opening night of their exhibition to promote British jewellery designers. He was filmed by British Pathé News on 17 November 1962 standing beside co-exhibitors Lilian Hall and Gilian Packard (see page 126).

His contemporaries might have breathed a sigh of relief when, after such a promising start, King chose to pursue a very successful career outside of the jewellery trade. In 1964, he formed what was to become the International Group of Companies, a family business involved in healthcare management, property development, sports marketing, leisure operations and packaging.

Examples of King's work can be seen in the permanent collection of jewellery at Goldsmiths' Hall.

---

1. "Man of the Month, Roger M King", *Goldsmith's Journal*, December 1961, p. 564.

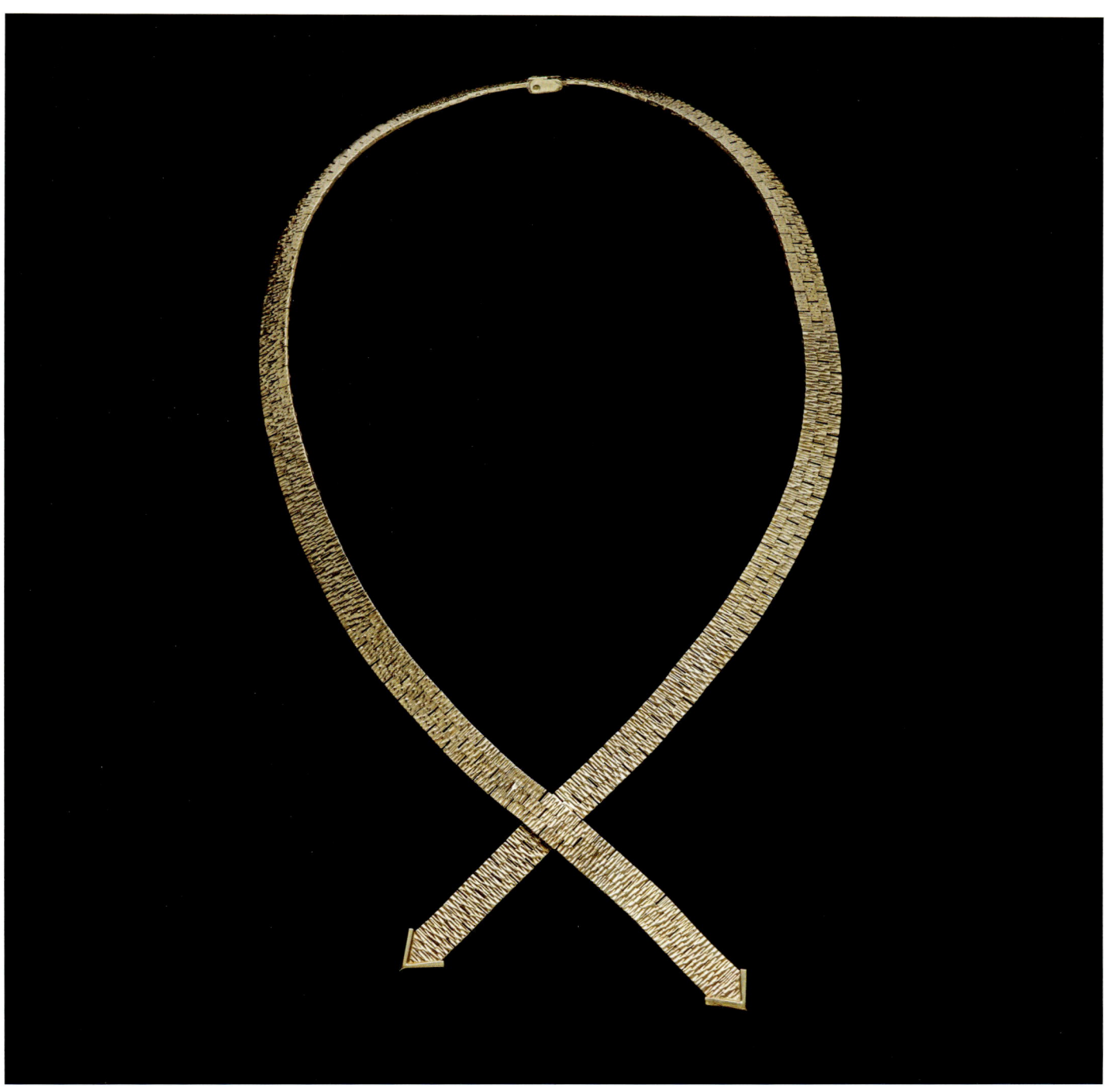

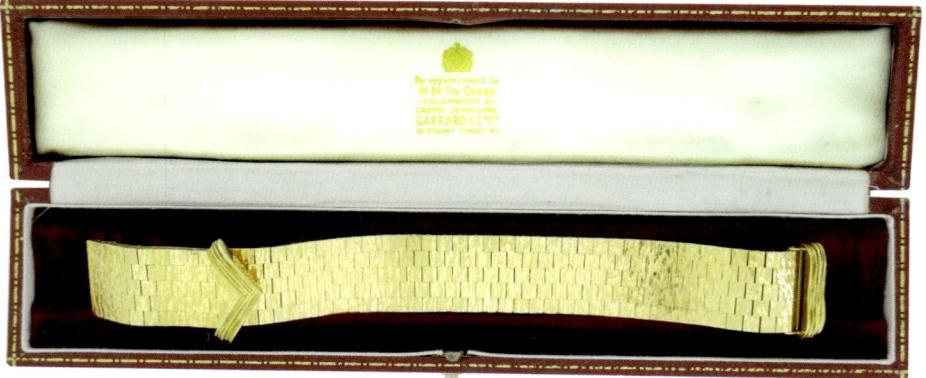

Previous page:
Necklace in 9ct gold, Roger King, c.1961

Above:
Necklace in 18ct gold, Roger King, 1972

Left:
18ct gold bracelet, Roger King, 1965. Cased by Garrard & Co.

Right:
Baguette diamond bracelet with five linked sections of platinum wire collets set with 164 articulated baguette diamonds, Roger King, maker's mark RMK, 1961. First prize DeBeers British Jewellery Competition 1961, section up to £2,750 value

103

18ct gold, cast flexible bar bracelet with enamel and 18 diamonds on textured background, Roger King, 1961; won first prize in De Beers British Jewellery Competition, 1961, in the section for items worth up to £750

Watch, with workings by Bueche-Girod, Roger King, 1963

Roy King
1913-2000

Roy Cecil King was an innovative watch and jewellery designer with a workshop in Watford. He began his career in 1927, aged 14, as apprentice to the Hatton Garden jewellery firm M J Greengross. King also attended night classes at the Sir John Cass Technical Institute, perfecting his skill at diamond mounting.

During the Second World War, King worked as a planning engineer in an aeroplane factory, eventually heading up a 100-strong department at the de Havilland Aircraft Company. There, he learnt machine tool techniques, which he would later use in the manufacture of his jewellery and watches.

After the war, King set up his workshop in Watford where he made every kind of jewellery, from tie pins to five strawberry-leaf tiaras for duchesses to wear at the coronation of HM The Queen in 1953.

When restrictions on the import of Swiss watch movements were lifted in 1960, King began to concentrate more on watchmaking and designing his own cases and bracelets. He rightly calculated that Swiss movements conferred a sense of quality that would prove popular with the general public and signed an exclusive contract with Bueche-Girod, the Swiss movement manufacturer.

In 1965, King built his own factory outside Watford where he employed 65 people to make 25,000 gold and silver pieces a year. He also designed "bark finish" on bracelets, watches and rings, which gained a certain amount of publicity in 1966 when Pattie Boyd wore one of his "bark finish" wedding rings during her marriage to Beatle, George Harrison.

In 1971, King won a National Export Council Award and became a Freeman of the City of London.[1] In the same year, he also made an 18ct gold watch with tiger's-eye dial. The textured open-hoop bracelet is a trademark of King's work.

In 1973, King purchased the Swiss watch company La Montre Royale de Geneve. The watches branded with this name were among the most luxurious ever produced, and proved especially popular in the Middle East.[2] Two of these watches, inscribed La Montre Royale, Geneva, were purchased in 1983 by The Worshipful Company of Goldsmiths and are in their permanent collection.

A year later, King was given a one-man show at Goldsmiths' Hall and took the opportunity to launch a new collection of silver watches. The watch shown opposite is almost certainly from this collection.[3] The inscription on the back of the watch reads: "This sterling silver watch by Roy King with a London assay mark has a date letter t for 1974". It is mechanically very basic, with a Swiss manual-wind movement, black hands on a square silver dial, no numerals and no date window, but with its original silver bracelet.

King opened a showroom in Mayfair in 1980, where he had a bench and continued to make one-off pieces for clients. He died in 2000, having witnessed the inclusion of several of his pieces in the 1999 Treasures of the 20th Century exhibition at Goldsmiths' Hall.

The clever thing about King was the balance he managed to strike between running a factory and his public image as an artist designer. To an extent, Andrew Grima achieved the same balance. Both designers understood that it was the star quality of their individual designs which attracted couture customers like nothing else could.

---

1. Roy King obituary, *Daily Telegraph*, 9 November 2000.
2. Christopher Ward forum. "Roy King and His Watches" 9 March 2019, www.christopherwardforum.com.
3. op.cit. *Daily Telegraph*.

Top:
Ladies' silver bangle watch, Roy King, 1974

Bottom:
18ct gold watch ring with tiger's-eye face, maker's mark RCK, signed Bueche-Girod, c.1970

Joseph, Paul and Roger Kutchinsky
1914-2000 / 1950-2000 / 1945-

The Kutchinsky jewellery business was founded in 1893 by Hirsch Kutchinsky, a Polish Jew who arrived in Britain with his family after fleeing persecution. He set up a jewellery manufacturing workshop in the East End of London with his son, Morris.

The Kutchinsky brand is probably best known for its jewellery production from the 1960s to the 1980s, which is why it is included in this book. Indeed, Kutchinsky jewels from the second half of the twentieth century are highly sought after today.

In 1958, Hirsch Kutchinsky's grandson, Joseph, moved the Kutchinsky shop from the East End to 73 Brompton Road in Knightsbridge. Kutchinsky's jewels were, after the constraints of the Second World War, generally large-scale, ostentatious and colourful pieces, often utilising semi-precious stones such as tiger's eye, coral, lapis and turquoise.

In 1961, Kutchinsky exhibited two pieces of jewellery at the International Exhibition of Modern Jewellery 1890-1961 at Goldsmiths' Hall. In his accompanying notes to the catalogue, Graham Hughes wrote that the workshop for Kutchinsky was Sannit & Stein Ltd[1] in Denman Street, London, where it remained for over 30 years, until the lease ran out.

James Miller, the master goldsmith, designed and made the Flax Flower Easter Egg for Kutchinsky in 1988 when he was working for Sannit & Stein. He had always been inspired by the work of Michael Perchin, one of Fabergé's master craftsmen. From then on, Miller and Sannit & Stein created several fine pieces for Kutchinsky.[2] This means that between 1960 and 1991, Sannit & Stein was the main workshop for Kutchinsky.

It is fair to say that Paul Kutchinsky, who, together with his brother Roger, had taken over the running of the family business in 1989, was obsessed with the work of Peter Carl Fabergé and the pieces he created for the Russian imperial family. Indeed, it was his fixation with the romance of the Fabergé legend that eventually contributed to the downfall of the house of Kutchinsky.

The idea of the Argyle Library Egg was hatched by Paul Kutchinsky, with whose name the egg will always be synonymous. The design was created by the master goldsmith and jewellery designer, Leo de Vroomen (see page 36). The egg was made at the De Vroomen Alexander workshop in Rosebery Avenue, London, by ex-McCabe McCarty craftsmen for a company set up by Leo de Vroomen and his business partner, Alexander Parkes. The "library" part of the egg is the rotating "surprise" when the egg is opened. The pink diamonds came from the Argyle Mining Company in Perth, Western Australia.

The Kutchinsky business was sold in 1991 to Hilton Jewels Ltd (alias Moussaieff Jewellers Ltd), but the shop remained in the Brompton Road until 2000. And the Argyle Library Egg? Well, it was last heard of (in 2013)[3] gracing the hall of the house belonging to a Japanese businessman in Tokyo.

---

1. Graham Hughes, *Modern Jewelry: An International Survey 1888-1967* (Studio Books, 1963), 237.
2. James Miller, *The Work of a Master Goldsmith: A Unique Collection* (Marlborough: NAG Press, 2009).
3. Serena Kutchinsky, "A Good Egg", *Sunday Times*, 16 June 2013.

Ruby, emerald and diamond brooch set with circular-cut rubies and emeralds within beaded border, maker's mark KLd, 1961

Left:
18ct gold diamond and ruby ring, stamped Kutchinsky, 1971

Right:
18ct yellow gold, diamond and ruby-set brooch and earclip suite modelled as a scrolled feather or plume, brilliant-cut diamonds with round-cut rubies, 1963

111

Hans Georg Mautner
1901-c.1972

Hans Georg Mautner was born in Weigelsdorf, Austria. He did an apprenticeship in Prague in 1919 and then went to work for the wholesale silversmiths and jewellers, Berthold Muller,[1] at Hanau,[2] in 1921. At the same time, he attended evening classes at the Hanau Art School.

Mautner established a workshop and retail shop in Vienna in 1925 and exhibited regularly at the Künstlerhaus[3] in Vienna. In his book, *Modern Jewelry*, Graham Hughes included a photograph of pieces shown by Mautner in Vienna in 1933.[4] The picture is interesting because the jewellery he exhibited is sculptural; clearly, Mautner's style changed after he came to work in London in 1938. Prior to that, he won a silver medal at the Milan Triennale[5] in 1933 and a gold medal at the Paris Exhibition in 1937.

According to his biography, which accompanied the catalogue for the 1961 International Exhibition of Modern Jewellery 1890-1961, Mautner had a workshop in Hatton Garden from 1938. This may well be true, but I have never come across any jewellery of his with a London assay mark dated earlier than 1952.

It may be that Mautner was unable to make any jewellery during the years of the Second World War. With Austria being an ally of Nazi Germany, he may have been interned. Whatever the reason, the important point is that Mautner lent five pieces to the International Exhibition of Modern Jewellery 1890-1961, one of which (catalogue no. 560), the gold cufflinks with groove, dated 1935, remains in the permanent collection at Goldsmiths' Hall.

Interestingly, four of the pieces exhibited by Mautner were made in Vienna in the 1920s and 1930s, and only one was made in London, in 1961. Of the four pieces that were made in Vienna, I believe that I may have found the gold and onyx brooch, dated 1928, which was exhibited in the catalogue (no. 537). The brooch, which has recently come into my possession, is a perfect illustration of Mautner's early sculptural work.

In the late 1950s and early 1960s, Mautner produced modest but beautifully made jewellery for S.J. Rood in Burlington Arcade and Boucheron in Old Bond Street, both in London. These pieces are now rare but a few still come up at auction. When they do, they will carry the marks of HGM and Boucheron and they will be London assay marked. Mautner also made jewellery for the Crown Jeweller, Garrard and Co. Ltd, from 1952, the year in which they merged with The Goldsmiths & Silversmiths Company and moved to their premises at 112 Regent Street, London.

Mautner worked in a similar style to Ben Rosenfeld (see page 136), using both 9 and 18ct yellow gold and semi-precious stones. Like Rosenfeld, he was prone to producing wacky animal brooches in whimsical poses, often using rubies or emeralds as eyes. The wackiest of them all brings us to Sid the Scorpion.

I found Sid the Scorpion in Cornwall (I am not called the 'rock hound' for nothing), lying on his back and waving his 9ct gold legs in the air in an abandoned way. He was made by Mautner at his most outlandish. His eyes are made from rubies and his body from a large, lilac-blue chalcedony stone. Apart from this, Sid is

---

1. Berthold Muller of Hanau subtly changed their name from Muller to Miller in 1915 when they became importers to the UK.
2. Hanau is a large town in Hesse, Germany, located 25km east of Frankfurt.
3. The Künstlerhaus is an art centre in Vienna, designed by August Weber and built between 1865 and 1868 by the Austrian Artists Society, the oldest surviving artist society in the country. The building was opened in September 1868.
4. Graham Hughes, *Modern Jewelry: An International Survey 1888-1967* (Studio Books, 1963), 47, plate 23.
5. The Triennale di Milano is a design and art exhibition in Milan in northern Italy.
6. *Antiques Roadshow*, first broadcast on the BBC in the UK on 4 August 2019.

pretty revolting to look at, but the important point is that he is dated 1960.

Mautner's brooches are normally small pieces designed in the style of the period, which was reluctant to draw attention to itself; the reverse of the bold brooches designed by Andrew Grima, for example, a little later in the 1960s and throughout the 1970s.

The exception to this rule is Mautner's rings, which were large by the standard of the day. He seems to have worked to a pattern, as many are of a similar rope design. He used different stones for variety but also used an 18ct yellow gold acanthus leaf design which is an attractive alternative style. Mautner's tree brooch was also a frequently repeated design, using different stones and sometimes different metals.

Shortly after I found Sid, I watched an edition of the BBC's *Antiques Roadshow*,[6] in which expert Geoffrey Munn examined a beautiful Fabergé brooch that had, as its central stone, a breathtaking lilac-blue chalcedony, set in yellow gold surrounded by diamonds. Munn, a very experienced Fabergé consultant, seemed surprised that Fabergé should choose such a low-value stone for a significant piece of jewellery when clearly he could afford the most expensive stones available. Munn eventually concluded that the brooch was a piece of art and was not necessarily about value. Chalcedony may be a worthless stone, but it has a stunning effect when it is set in yellow gold and used as the central feature in a piece of jewellery. Both Mautner and Fabergé understood this.

18ct gold diamond and sapphire ring, with nine sapphires, six diamonds of bombe-design, openwork lattice to rope-twist decoration, maker's mark HGM, 1971

114

Far left:
18ct gold citrine and diamond ring, cluster of round and oval-cut Madeira citrines with diamond accents with textured gold leaf motifs, maker's mark HGM, 1970

Left:
18ct gold diamond and coral ring, set within a border of Swiss-cut diamonds centrally set with round cabochon coral, 11mm in diameter, maker's mark HGM, 1972

Right:
18ct yellow gold textured brooch set with diamonds, emeralds, rubies and sapphires, maker's mark HGM, 1968

Far left:
Citrine and diamond brooch in 18ct yellow gold, set with a cluster of round and oval-cut Madeira citrines with diamond accents, maker's mark HGM, 1966

Above:
18ct yellow gold earrings set with a cluster of round and oval-cut Madeira citrines with diamonds, maker's mark HGM, 1964

Left:
Pair of 18ct yellow gold diamond earrings of multi-rope twist form, with three round brilliant-cut diamonds set centrally, maker's mark HGM, 1963

Left:
18ct yellow gold cabochon stone fish brooch, maker's mark HGM, 1962

Right:
9ct yellow gold pendant set around a natural blue chalcedony cabochon stone with red ruby eyes, maker's mark HGM, 1960; aka 'Sid the Scorpion'!

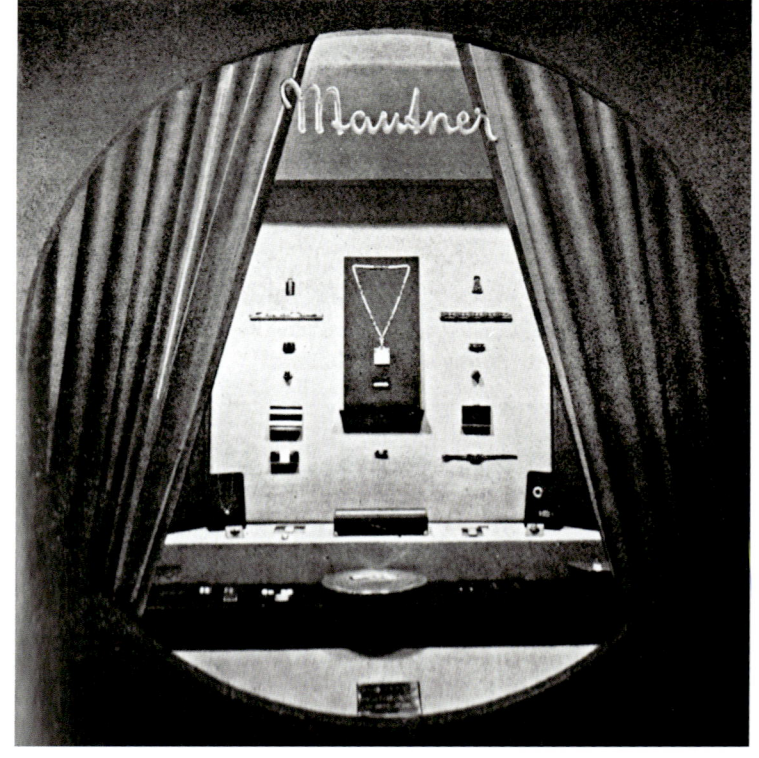

Above:
Onyx and gold brooch, thought to be the one shown in the International Exhibition of Modern Jewellery 1890-1961, maker's mark HM Vienna, c.1928

Right:
Mautner's shop window in Künstlerhaus, Vienna, 1933, showing similar brooches on display

18ct gold sapphire and diamond rope-twist brooch with matching earrings, maker's mark HGM, fitted case by Garrard & Co. Ltd, Crown Jewellers, 1954

David Morris
b.1936

David Morris started his apprenticeship at the age of 15, in London's famous Hatton Garden jewellery district, before going on to the Central School of Arts and Crafts where he graduated in 1962. In the same year, he opened a workshop in Hatton Garden, and in 1963 he and his design partner won the ninth De Beers Diamonds International Award. Morris won the award again the following year, a remarkable achievement for a "newbie".

From a collector's point of view, the pieces of jewellery made by David Morris in the late 1960s and early 1970s are probably amongst the most interesting of the era, in terms of design and craftsmanship.

In 1969, Morris moved from his workshop base in Hatton Garden to open his first Mayfair showroom on Conduit Street, London. There, for the next two decades, he expanded and extended his brand to cover outlets in Moscow, the Middle East and Paris, with additional boutiques in department stores such as Harrods.

Morris became known as the "James Bond Jeweller", with his company creating iconic pieces for the classic 007 films *Diamonds Are Forever* (1971), *The Man with the Golden Gun* (1974) and *Tomorrow Never Dies* (1997). Somewhat appropriately, David Morris lived up to this name by moving into 180 New Bond Street in 1996, choosing a magnificent town house that remains the company's flagship headquarters and on-site atelier. Morris's son, Jeremy, joined the company in 2003 and has inherited his father's passion for design and craftsmanship. He has since become CEO and creative director of the company.

In early 2020, David Morris opened a boutique in Bergdorf Goodman in New York.

David Morris jewels are on permanent display at the V&A, London, and in private collections all over the world. Their famous clients, past and present, include Elizabeth Taylor, HRH Princess Margaret, Empress Farah Pahlavi of Iran, Queen Noor of Jordan and the Duke and Duchess of Cambridge.

123

Left:
18ct gold and sapphire diamond wheat sheaf brooch, maker's mark DM, 1970

Above:
18ct gold diamond ring, maker's mark DM, 1971

Louis Osman
1914-1996

Louis Osman showed a flair for creativity even as a youth, channelling his talent into his training at The Bartlett School of Architecture and studying drawing at the Slade School of Fine Art.

Graham Hughes championed Louis Osman from the first, describing him as "an architect, goldsmith, draftsman, art historian and art patron"; most of all, according to Hughes, he was "a creator of genius".[1]

In 1961, Osman exhibited two pieces at Goldsmiths' Hall in London, at the International Exhibition of Modern Jewellery 1890-1961, and he also exhibited a beautiful diamond and gold spider's web necklace at the International Jewellery Exhibition in Tokyo in the same year. The necklace is now held in the permanent collection of jewellery at Goldsmiths' Hall.

Osman began his career as an architect. He made his name when he rebuilt the bomb-damaged Convent of the Holy Child Jesus on Cavendish Square in London, and followed this with his architectural tour-de-force, a Neo-Renaissance plate glass palazzo, the Principal's Lodgings, for Newnham College, Cambridge.

In the early 1960s, no doubt encouraged by Hughes, Osman left the world of masonry to work full time as a goldsmith and jeweller. He set up a workshop at Canons Ashby in Northamptonshire, employing a handful of silversmiths and other jewellery trades.

Under Hughes' direction, The Worshipful Company of Goldsmiths commissioned Osman to design a new treasury for Lincoln Cathedral, and then, in 1969, to make the crown that the Goldsmith's Company presented to Charles, Prince of Wales for his investiture at Caernarfon Castle – "the best-known piece of new British gold of [the] century".[2] In 1971, the Goldsmiths' Company held the Louis Osman Gold Exhibition at Goldsmiths' Hall, comprising 105 pieces, mostly new and modelled in gold. Besides the pieces produced for exhibitions, much of Osman's work was undertaken for private commissions.

Whether designing a building or a bracelet or a bowl, Osman loved to test techniques to their limits and revelled in the distinctive properties of precious metals, only working with them in their purest forms. The very distinctive track-link bracelet (see opposite) was made for a client in 1977, using Britannia silver and 22ct gold, also known as electrum. Electrum is a composite of gold, usually found occurring naturally, with a percentage of silver and sometimes copper. Britannia silver is an alloy containing 95.833 per cent silver. It is softer than sterling silver, an alloy containing 92.5 per cent silver. According to the auctioneer who sold the bracelet, the vendor was a dentist who originally supplied the gold to Osman. If this is the case, it is something to chew over. Gold has been used in dentistry for more than 4,000 years, and although crowns, fillings and bridges are usually made of 16ct gold (the metal has to be soft enough to mould but hard enough to bite on), they can be made of any gold that the client wants.

---

1. Graham Hughes, "Obituary: Louis Osman", *Independent*, 16 April 1996.
2. ibid.

22ct gold and Britannia silver track-link bracelet, 1977

Gilian Packard
1938-1997

Gilian Elizabeth Packard was born in Newcastle-upon-Tyne. The story goes that her father could not spell, so when he registered her birth, he spelt Gillian with one "l" rather than two. After she left school, Packard studied at the Kingston School of Art, the Central School of Arts and Crafts and the Royal College of Art. She won many awards and was one of the leading jewellery designers of the 1960s. Her pieces were sold at Richard Ogden in Burlington Arcade, Cameo Corner in Bloomsbury and many other leading retail outlets, including Hamilton & Inches in Edinburgh. Packard was also one of the little band of jewellers whom Graham Hughes escorted to trade shows all over Europe and the USA in the 1960s, waving the flag for Britain.

In addition to winning awards for her work, Packard was Professor of Jewellery and Silversmithing at the Glasgow School of Art and then at the Sir John Cass Department of Silversmithing, Jewellery and Applied Arts at London Guildhall University. In 1963 and 1964, Packard won De Beers Diamonds International Awards.

Packard exhibited one piece – an enamel and copper necklace dated 1959 – at the International Exhibition of Modern Jewellery 1890-1961 (no. 613 in the catalogue). This is interesting because she only experimented with the art of enamel in the early years of her career before abandoning it entirely.

Packard tended to use rough crystals as the central stone in her necklaces and brooches, with small diamonds as a lean accompaniment. She was, perhaps, less of a jeweller in the sense that she rarely used fine jewels in her work, and more of a designer craftsperson. Indeed, she was known to wear very little jewellery herself. The exceptions were her wedding ring (she married in 1965) and her emerald engagement ring. In a British Pathé News film entitled "Jewel of the Year", made for an important jewellery exhibition at Christie's auction house in 1962, she is seen wearing – shock horror! – a brooch, albeit a very plain one!

The Watermelon tourmaline necklace (see opposite), made by Packard in 1970, is worked in 14ct gold textured triangular links, matching the shape of the watermelon tourmalines. It is sprinkled with tiny blue zircons and is an immensely wearable piece of jewellery to this day.

Most of Packard's work was commissioned by private clients. A very wearable pendant necklace, made in 1967, is one such example (see page 130). The pear-shaped rhodochrosite stone is held within a two-colour, 18ct gold polished and textured bar and nugget-style setting. The pendant is suspended from a similarly textured and polished gold-bar panel necklace with gold nugget-style spacers between. It is bang in fashion today, more than 50 years after it was made.

In 1971, Packard became the first female Freeman of The Worshipful Company of Goldsmiths in a professional capacity. Examples of her work can be found in the permanent collection at Goldsmiths' Hall and at the V&A, London, where her pioneering interlocking engagement ring is one of the permanent exhibits. Packard died in 1997 at the comparatively young age of 59.

Watermelon tourmaline and 14ct gold necklace, alternately set with watermelon tourmalines and matching textured gold triangular links, maker's mark GEP, 1970

128

Left:
18ct gold citrine cocktail ring in a geometric mount and shank, maker's mark GEP, 1967

Right:
18ct yellow gold rose quartz pendant with five marquise-set diamonds, maker's mark GEP, 1968

130

Left:
18ct two-colour gold rhodochrosite crystal pendant, with pear-shaped panel with two-colour gold bar and nugget-style setting, maker's mark GEP, 1967

Right:
18ct gold brooch with white crystallised agate, maker's mark GEP, 1970

Wendy Ramshaw CBE
1939-2018

Born and educated in Sunderland, Wendy Anne Jopling Ramshaw studied illustration and fabric design at the College of Art and Industrial Design in Newcastle-upon-Tyne in the late 1950s. She went on to study for a teaching diploma at Reading University, 1960-1961, where she met artist and sculptor, David Watkins. The pair married in 1962.

Ramshaw did not exhibit at the International Exhibition of Modern Jewellery 1890-1961, but she was discovered by Graham Hughes shortly afterwards and he began collecting her work for the permanent collection at Goldsmiths' Hall.

Her paper earrings hit the market at Mary Quant's Bazaar in the early 1960s, modelled by the aptly named "Twiggy", and the publicity that these created put Ramshaw well on the road to fame with the media who were always looking for another jewellery design sensation. In about 1965, Ramshaw created her signature series of stacking rings displayed on a Perspex stand, which ultimately won her the Design Council Award for creative innovation in 1972. She was made a Freeman of The Worshipful Company of Goldsmiths in 1973 and was awarded a CBE in the same year.

Ramshaw's style was uniquely her own. She pushed the boundaries – and found fame – with her innovative designs, making pieces of jewellery with materials that ranged from semi and precious stones to glass, paper, porcelain, Perspex and plastic. There was usually very little value in the materials she used.

She had more than 30 solo exhibitions around the globe, from 1977, including three major exhibitions held jointly with her husband. In 1982, a retrospective exhibition was held at the V&A, London, organised by Sir Roy Strong. It celebrated Ramshaw's collaboration with Wedgwood and featured ceramics produced to Ramshaw's designs.

18ct gold pin with red Perspex, onyx and jasper,
maker's mark WR, 1978

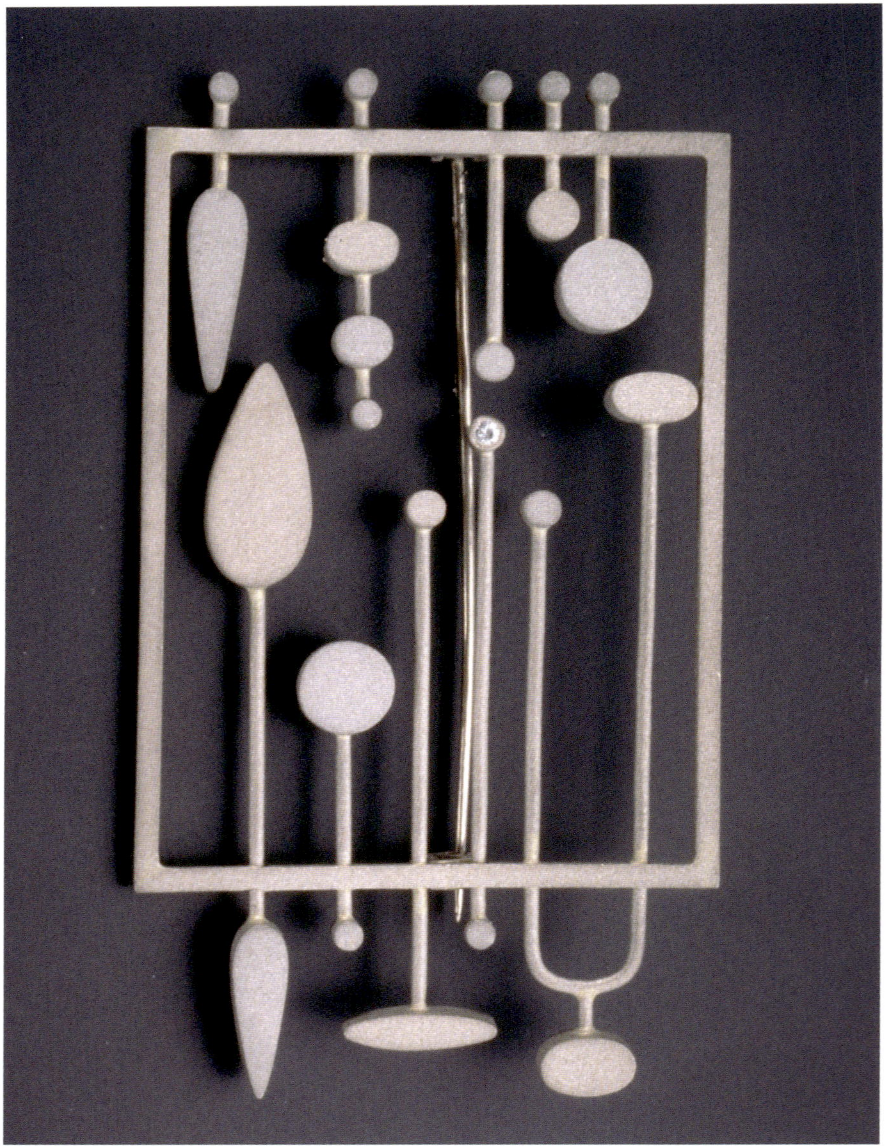

Left:
Ring set, 18ct gold, enamel, chrysoprase, tourmaline and acrylic, 1972

Above:
Brooch, 18ct white gold and diamond, 1972

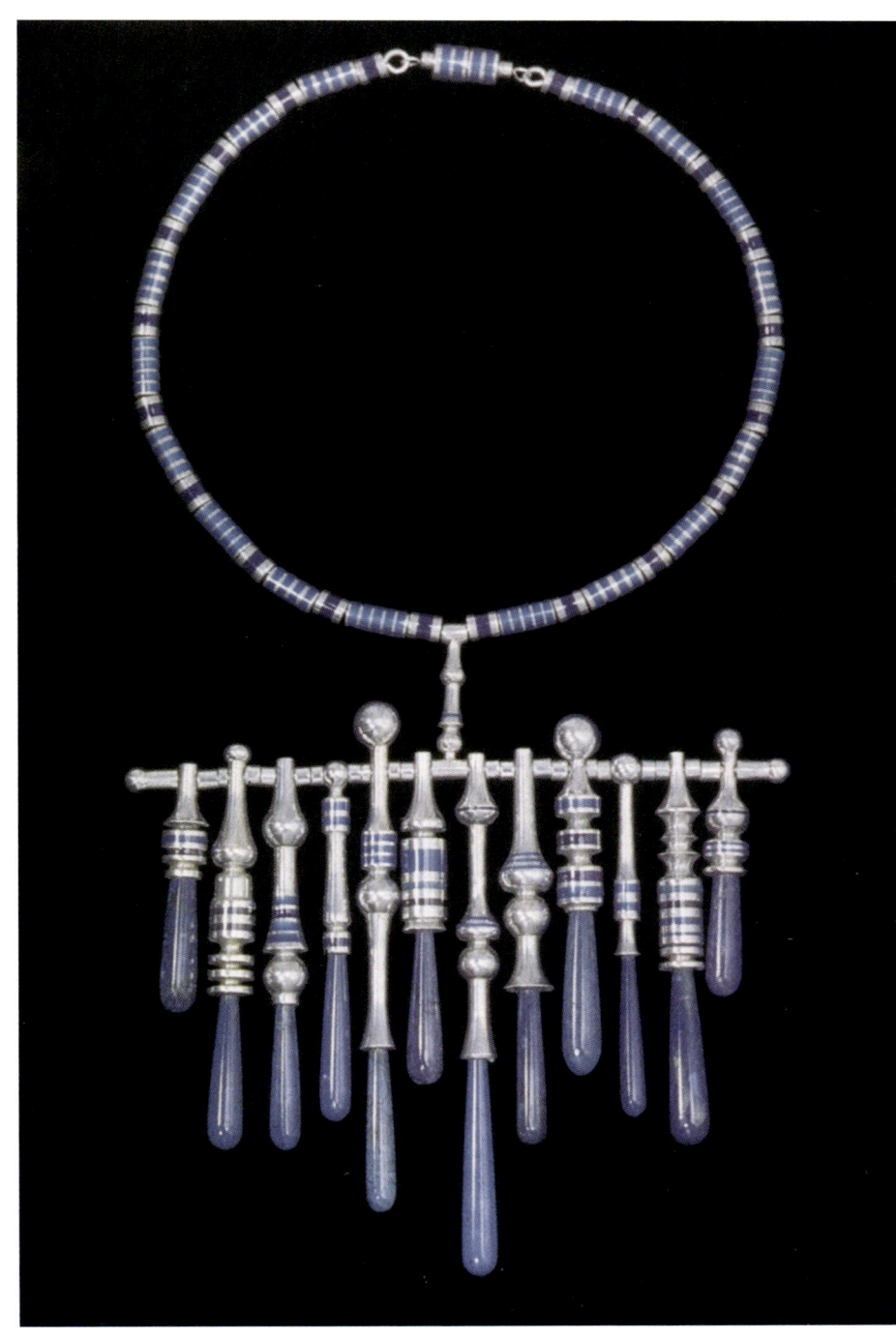

Necklace with blue enamel and lapis lazuli pendants, 1971

Ben Rosenfeld
c.1912-1981

Ben Rosenfeld was a talented jewellery designer and maker active between the years 1950 and 1977. He never had a retail shop, working instead out of his workshop at Rose Diamond House, 10 Hatton Garden, as Ben Rosenfeld (Jewels) Ltd. His maker's stamp is BR Ltd.

Rosenfeld was the founding father of the Variety Club Sandown Race Day, which raised funds on a grand scale, and served as Chief Barker (the elected Chair of the Board of Trustees at the Variety Club) in 1972.[1] In the past 60 years, the Variety Club has raised over £200 million and helped more than a million sick, disadvantaged and disabled children. Unsurprisingly, many of Rosenfeld's jewellery clients were from the world of entertainment and he had an international following.

Rosenfeld was a close friend of film producer Nat Cohen, with whom he formed a racehorse-owning partnership. They won the 1962 Grand National with Kilmore, a 28/1 shot ridden in Nat Cohen's colours by Fred Winter and trained by Ryan Price at Findon, Sussex.

Rosenfeld's jewellery was unusual for its liberal use of precious stones at a time, in the 1960s and 1970s, when they were expensive to purchase. He never stinted. When many designers were using more gold and cutting back on the number of precious stones, he did the reverse, probably because his clients wanted them and had the means to pay.

Rosenfeld died in 1981, following a stroke. His work is represented in the V&A, London.

---

1. varietyclub.org.uk, accessed on 22 February 2021.

Gem-set gold fish brooch set with circular-cut diamonds, a sapphire collar and turquoise cabochon eye, in 18ct yellow gold, maker's mark BRLd, 1962

138

18ct gold and diamond brooch and earrings, designed as a textured foliate spray with single and brilliant-cut diamonds, maker's mark BRLd, 1968

139

18ct yellow gold brooch and earrings, designed as stylised pencil shavings and set with circular-cut diamonds and rubies, maker's mark BRLd, 1964

140

Ruby and diamond bracelet, formed as a series of bombe rope-twist links, each set with circular-cut rubies or brilliant-cut diamonds, maker's mark BRLd, 1965

18ct gold, ruby and diamond bracelet, maker's mark BRLd, 1962

Tom Scott
b.1946

Tom Edward Scott, the master goldsmith, trained at Hornsey College of Art under Ron Stevens, Keith Redfern, Gerda Flöckinger and his mentor and friend, Ernest Blyth, graduating in 1968.

My first meeting with Scott involved little more than knocking on his studio door to ask if he would sign a ring he had made in 1969, as part of a demi-parure I had acquired. A parure is a full set of matching jewellery that is intended to be worn all together. A demi-parure describes any set of jewellery that comprises two or more matching pieces. The problem with parures or demi-parures, which had been so popular in the first half of the twentieth century and, indeed, since the seventeenth century, is that few people in the second half of the twentieth century (let alone the twenty-first century) could afford to buy them. As a result, many parures were split up by dealers, the beautiful fitted cases discarded, and each item in the set sold individually, often for more money than the entire set would fetch.

That was one problem. The second problem was that because the jewellery had been made as a set, usually only the main pieces were signed and dated by the original maker or designer. The accompanying pieces that had not been signed, like the earrings, brooches or rings (in my case), lost their identity once they were severed from the set and swallowed into the vast, anonymous jewellery market. I had the necklace, which was clearly signed and dated by Scott, but the ring was unmarked and needed its own identity. Fortunately for me, Scott was immensely approachable and happily signed the ring for me.

Since that first meeting, I have got to know Scott very well. The stairs up to his workshop are still hazardous, the workshop is in a time warp and the tools could have been used in Pliny's day.

It is pretty much common knowledge that Scott worked for Andrew Grima from 1968 until 2007. He still works for the Grima brand now, which is run by Grima's widow, Jojo, and their daughter, Francesca. Less well known is the fact that Scott has always designed and made jewellery under his own name, selling it either through outlets like Cameo Corner and Wartski, or through private commissions. He has always preferred to make – rather than market – jewellery, which is why he is less well known than he should be.

Scott once asked if he could make me a ring. When I told him that I only purchased vintage pieces, he said, "But how can anything become vintage if it wasn't contemporary to start with?" "Good point, Tom," I found myself saying. And so, the most beautiful ring was born.

On another occasion, I had been fortunate – or so I thought – in finding a cabochon green chalcedony and diamond ring, signed by Scott. The ring, which was set in 18ct gold and dated 1969 by the London Assay Office, had a pair of matching earrings. Delighted with my purchase, I showed the demi-parure to Scott. He looked carefully at the ring and the earrings. Eventually, he said slowly, "The ring is mine, but it has been remodelled. The beautiful faceted ruby has been replaced by the chalcedony stone, which has been set carelessly into the hole left by the ruby. Can you see the minute gap?" I could, and that afternoon I learnt a sharp lesson in observation. I should have studied the pieces more carefully and looked for the maker's quality, which clearly wasn't there, before I made the purchase. "The earrings," Scott added, "are nothing to do with me and were obviously made by an unknown hand to match the ring." Fortunately, I was able to return the set to the original vendor, who was as shocked as I was. No harm done, except for bruised egos!

Scott's work is in the collection of The Worshipful Company of Goldsmiths, London.

18ct gold citrine and diamond collar pendant necklace and matching ring, maker's mark TES, dated 1969

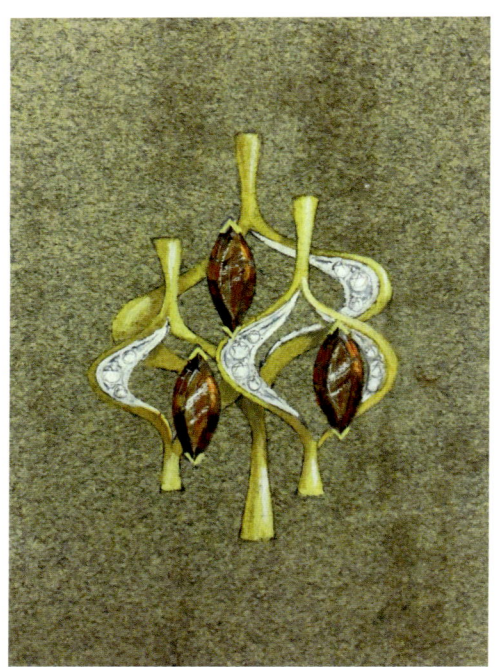

Anti-clockwise from top left:
Brooch, forged 18ct yellow gold motives with white gold diamond ribbons and set with three navette citrines, c.1970-73

Brooch pendant and chain, drawn gold tube with radiating ribs set with brilliant diamonds, c.1970-73

Ring, fine tanzanite set in yellow gold with diamond-set platinum ribbons, c.1970-73

Pendant and chain, drawn gold tube set with large aquamarine and diamond highlights, c.1970-73

Anti-clockwise from top left:
Ring and earrings, drawn gold tube set with navette aquamarines and brilliant diamonds, c.1970-73

Brooch, gold ribbons with fine tube detail and set with brilliant diamonds, c.1970-73

Ring, unusually cut green tourmaline, yellow gold and brilliant diamonds, c.1970-73

Brooch, "spider web" radiating vanes with interlaced planes set with brilliant diamonds, c.1970-73

David Thomas
b.1938

Described in the 1961 catalogue of the International Exhibition of Modern Jewellery 1890-1961 as a "jeweller, silversmith", David Arthur Thomas studied at the Twickenham School of Art from 1955 to 1958. He won a scholarship to the Royal College of Art, where he achieved the title of Royal Scholar by the end of his first year. Encouraged by this, he set up his own workshop in 1960, whilst still a student at the RCA.

The three pieces of jewellery – a bracelet (plate 81 in the catalogue of the International Exhibition of Modern Jewellery 1890-1961), a pendant necklace and earrings (respectively, catalogue numbers 766, 767 and 768) – contributed by Thomas to the International Exhibition in 1961 were all made in silver and are now in the collection at Goldsmiths' Hall. In 1972, De Beers released their Atlantis collection of diamond jewellery featuring pieces by David Thomas and John Donald (see page 48).

Not long ago, I bought a brooch by Thomas at a small auction house in Dorset. Mould covered the brooch box, which, after careful cleaning, revealed itself as one of Thomas's early green leather-backed cases, with his name and shop address printed in black on the white silk lining of the lid. The 18ct gold and pearl brooch inside was date-marked 1965 and, by some miracle, was almost none the worse for wear, despite its damp storage.

A leading jewellery designer and maker, Thomas opened his shop at 42 Old Church Street, London, in 1965, the same year he made this brooch. In 1984, he moved to his present shop at 65 Pimlico Road, London, where he has welcomed clients ever since.

I took the brooch I bought in Dorset to Thomas to be cleaned. It was tricky because whilst the gold had oxidised quite badly, the pearls, which sat in the gold cups, were in wonderful shape. Indeed, one wondered whether, in some weird way, the damp storage had been of benefit to them! David did a grand job restoring the gold to its former lustre but there was nothing he could do about the mouldy smell in the green velvet and silk interior of the box. Every time I open the box, the smell reminds me of the perils of bad storage. Of course, I could replace the lining but that would spoil the magic.

Thomas has been a Liveryman of The Worshipful Company of Goldsmiths since 1982. His work is represented in the collections at Goldsmiths' Hall and the V&A, London.

147

18ct yellow gold brooch of pearls set in small gold cups, maker's mark DAT, 1965

148

18ct gold necklace, with a pendant from which
22 drops fall, each with a pearl, 1965

18ct yellow and white gold necklace with rough rock crystal bar, 1966

18ct gold necklace set with red agate, flanked on each side by seven diamonds, 1975

151

18ct gold synthetic corundum ring, maker's mark DAT, 1972

George Weil
b.1938

I bought the George Weil ring on page 153 (opposite) from E.S. Campbell to celebrate the opening of Footnote, my designer shoe shop in the King's Road, Chelsea, in 1967. At the time, I had no idea who George Weil was, but Mr Campbell was promoting him as an up-and-coming jewellery designer and maker, and assured me that we would be hearing a lot more from him in the future. The ring is signed and, in keeping with a great deal of Weil's work, does not carry an assay mark. I always found this odd, given that Weil worked out of Hatton Garden, which is dominated by the London Assay Office. How difficult would it have been to pay the office a visit occasionally?

I cannot recall how much the ring cost, since I have carelessly lost the receipt, but I do remember thinking that I could just about afford it. Weil's ring has remained a treasured possession for more than 50 years. I also have the box it was retailed in as an important memento. This is fortunate because Mr Campbell has not had his shop in Sloane Street for a very long time. Keeping receipts and boxes as added provenance is something I would urge all collectors to make a habit of.

George Weil was born in Vienna in 1938. In 1939, his family fled to England from Antwerp, just before the start of the Second World War. Not much is known about Weil's early life, except that he briefly attended Saint Martins School of Art in 1956, and later went on to work out of Hatton Garden, but the ring speaks for itself as a beautiful work of art using 18ct gold and diamonds.

Many of Weil's jewellery pieces are sculptural in design, almost always worked in 18ct yellow gold (sometimes textured) and set with precious stones. Weil worked in a traditional style but was not totally immune to the 1960s fashion of using raw stones in jewellery.

George Weil also made pieces of jewellery for Galerie Jean Renet, which opened at 1 Old Bond Street, London, in 1969. An exhibition of his work was held between 1 and 9 July 1971.[1]

According to Mahnaz Ispahani, founder and CEO of the Mahnaz Collection in New York, Weil sold his jewellery business in London in 1979 and made no more jewellery. Instead, he entered the mysterious world of Japanese netsuke art, initially as a collector and then as a maker. He now lives in Israel. The V&A in London has examples of his jewellery in its collection.

---

1. *Design Journal*, issue No. 271, July 1971

Above:
Garnet and diamond brooch with abstract yellow gold surround, maker's mark G. Weil, 1970s

Left:
18ct gold ring set with seven circular-cut diamonds, maker's mark G. Weil, c.1965

Bibliography

Bonhams. 2017. *Fine Jewellery: Including a Private Collection of Jewels by Grima*. London: Bonhams.
Cartlidge, Barbara. 1985. *Twentieth-Century Jewelry*. New York: Harry N. Abrahams.
Chadour-Sampson, Beatriz and Hosegood, Janice. 2016. *Barbara Cartlidge and Electrum Gallery: A Passion for Jewellery*. Stuttgart: Arnoldsche Art.
Christie's, *Property from the Collection of Her Royal Highness The Princess Margaret, Countess of Snowdon. Vol 1: Jewellery and Fabergé* (London: Christie's, 2006).
Cox, Caroline. 2010. *Vintage Jewellery*. Glasgow: Carlton Books.
De Vroomen. 2017. London: De Vroomen Designs Ltd.
Devlin, Carole and Simkin, Victoria Kate, eds. 2018. *Stuart Devlin: Designer, Goldsmith, Silversmith*. Woodbridge; ACC Art Books.
Donald, John and Casselton Elliott, Russell. 2015. *Precious Statements: John Donald, Designer and Jeweller*. Carmarthen: McNidder & Grace.
Edwards, Rod. 1977. *The Technique of Jewellery*. London: B.T. Batsford.
Gage, Elizabeth. 2003. *The Unconventional Gage: A Book of Unique Jewellery Design*. London: New Gate Press.
Grant, William. 2020. *Andrew Grima: The Father of Modern Jewellery*. Woodbridge: ACC Art Books.
Grima, Andrew and The Worshipful Company of Goldsmiths. 1991. *Grima: Retrospective*. London: The Goldsmiths' Company.
Grima, Andrew. 1969. *About Time*. Biel/Bienne, Switzerland: Omega Watch Co.
Guinness, Louisa. 2017. *Art as Jewellery: From Calder to Kapoor*. Woodbridge: ACC Art Books.
Hughes, Graham. 1963. "The New Jewellers", in *The Saturday Book*, ed. John Hadfield. London: Hutchinson.
Hughes, Graham. 1963. *Modern Jewelry: An International Survey 1888-1967*. New York: Studio Books.
Hughes, Graham. 1972. *The Art of Jewelry*. New York: Studio Books.
Hughes, Graham. 2003. *Grima: A Jeweller's World*. San Francisco: Starcity.
International Exhibition of Modern Jewellery 1890-1961. 1961. London: The Worshipful Company of Goldsmiths.
Ispahani Bartos, Mahnaz. 2018. *London Originals: The Jeweler's Art in Radical Times*. Mahnaz Collection.
Miller, James. 2009. *The Work of a Master Goldsmith: A Unique Collection*. Marlborough: NAG Press.
Newby Haspeslagh, Martine. 2017. *Jewelry by Contemporary Painters and Sculptors @50: 1967-2017*. London: Didier.
Ransome Wallis, Rosemary. 1985. *Recent Acquisitions by The Goldsmiths' Company 1975-1985*. London: The Goldsmiths' Company.
Ransome Wallis, Rosemary. 2000. *Treasures of the 20th Century*. London: Goldsmiths' Company.
Sancroft-Baker, Raymond and Hue-Williams, Sarah. 2016. *Hidden Gems*. Greensboro, North Carolina: Unicorn Press.
Stardust, The Art of British Jewellery in the 1960s. 2019. London: Lyon & Turnbull.
Usselman, Melvyn C. 2015. *Pure Intelligence: The Life of William Hyde Wollaston*. Chicago: University of Chicago Press.
Willsberger, Johann, comp. 1991. *GRIMA*.
Wingfield, Mary Ann. 2020. *Anything Is Possible*. MAW Designs.
Wollaston, T.C. 1924. *Opal, The Gem of the Never Never*. London: Thomas Murby & Co.

Acknowledgements

I would like to thank everybody who helped me to make this book a reality. In particular my long-suffering editor, Andrew Whittaker, who boosted my spirits when I was flagging. My enterprising PA, Matt Watkins, who juggled our day job with countless literary demands. Alice Whately, for her patience in proofreading the raw text. Lord Snowdon who undertook to write the Foreword with enthusiasm and good humour. The jewellery designers and their relations who shared their stories and answered my numerous questions with tolerance. The auction houses, the Museums and The Worshipful Company of Goldsmiths, without whose help my task would have been far greater, and finally, but by no means least, my family who have supported me and encouraged me throughout.

Image Credits

Page 2, Andrew Grima pendant/brooch – Private collection, Photo Jon Stokes

Page 4, Gillian Packard brooch – Private collection, Photo Jon Stokes

Page 5, Hans Georg Mautner ring – Private collection, Photo Jon Stokes

Page 7, Andrew Grima ring – Private collection, Photo Jon Stokes

Page 9, Andrew Grima pendant, Munsteiner stone – Private collection, Photo Francesca Grima

Page 10, Frances Beck ring – Private collection, Photo MAW Designs Ltd

Page 10, Kutchinsky pendant – Private collection, Photo MAW Designs Ltd

Page 11, David Morris brooch – Private collection, Photo Jon Stokes

Page 13, John Donald brooch and earrings – Private collection, Photo Jon Stokes

Page 15, *Vogue* front cover with Grima ring – Photo David Bailey/Vogue © The Condé Nast Publications Ltd.

Page 16, Prince of Wales' Investiture Coronet by Louis Osman – Photo The Royal Collection Trust

Pages 18, 19, Kutchinsky brooch and earring set – Private collection, Photos Jon Stokes

Page 20, Frances Beck and Ernest Blyth – Photo from *Goldsmiths' Guide*

Page 21, Frances Beck brooch – Private collection, Photo Jon Stokes

Page 22, Ernest Blyth brooch – Private collection, Photo Jon Stokes

Page 24, Gerald Benney ring – Private collection, Photo MAW Designs Ltd

Page 25, Gerald Benney brooch – Collection: The Worshipful Company of Goldsmiths

Page 27, Ingeborg Bratman ring – Private collection, Photo Jon Stokes

Page 29, Jocelyn Burton brooch – Private collection, Photo Ian Moore

Pages 30, 32, 33, Jocelyn Burton sketches – Private collection, Photography Ian Moore

Page 35, Charles de Temple rings – Private collection, Photo Jon Stokes

Page 37, Le de Vroomen ring and bracelet – Private collection, Photo Jon Stokes

Pages 38, 39, 40, 41, Leo de Vroomen – Private collection

Page 43, Stuart Devlin brooch and ring – Private collection, Photo Jon Stokes

Pages 44, 45, Stuart Devlin ring and brooch – Private collection, Photos MAW Designs Ltd

Pages 46, 47, Stuart Devlin brooches – courtesy Carole Devlin

Page 49, John Donald ring – Private collection, Photo Jon Stokes

Pages 50–51, 52, 54, 55, John Donald pieces – Private collection, Photos Jon Stokes

Page 53, John Donald advert – Private collection

Page 57, Rod Edwards brooch – Photo John Kelly

Pages 58, 59, Rod Edwards necklace – Private collection, Photo Jon Stokes

Pages 61, 62, Gerda Flöckinger necklace – Private collection, Photo Jon Stokes

Pages 65, 66, 67, Elizabeth Gage pieces – Private collection, Photos Prudence Cuming Ltd

Pages 69, 70, 71, 72 73, Alan Gard pieces – Private collection, Photos Jon Stokes

Pages 74, 75, 76, Michael Gosschalk portrait and pieces – Private collection

Page 77, Michael Gosschalk brooch – Private collection, Photo Jon Stokes

Pages 79, 80, 81, 82, 84, 85, 86, 87, 88, 89, 90, 91, 93, Andrew Grima pieces – Private collection, Photos Jon Stokes

Page 92, Andrew Grima brooch/pendant – Private collection, Photo MAW Designs Ltd

Page 94, Alfred Gruber in the workshop – Private collection

Page 96, Alfred Gruber brooch – Private collection, Photo Jon Stokes

Pages 95, 97, 98 (above left, left), 99, Jacqueline Stieger pieces – Private collection, Photos R&R Studio

Page 98 (above), Jacqueline Stieger orange moonstone brooch – Private collection, Photo Gerardine Mulcahy

Pages 101, 102 (above), 103, 104, 105, Roger King pieces – Collection: The Worshipful Company of Goldsmiths

Page 102 (left), Roger King bracelet in case – Private collection, Photo MAW Designs Ltd

Page 107, Roy King watches – Private collection, Photo MAW Designs Ltd

Pages 109, 110, 111, Kutchinsky – Private collection, Photos Jon Stokes

Pages 113, 114, 115, 116, 117, 118, 119, Hans Georg Mautner – Private collection, Photos Jon Stokes

Page 120 (above), 121, Hans Georg Mautner pieces – Private collection, Photo MAW Designs Ltd

Page 123, David Morris pieces – Private collection, Photo Jon Stokes

Page 125, Louis Osman bracelet – Private collection, Photo Jon Stokes

Pages 127, 128, 129, 130, 131, Gillian Packard pieces – Private collection, Photos Jon Stokes

Page 133, Wendy Ramshaw pin – Private collection, Photo Jon Stokes

Pages 134, 135, Wendy Ramshaw pieces – Collection: The Worshipful Company of Goldsmiths

Page 136, Ben Rosenfeld – photograph courtesy of Variety, the Children's Charity (formerly the Variety Club of Great Britain)

Pages 137, 138, 139, 140, Ben Rosenfeld pieces – Private collection, Photo Jon Stokes

Page 141, Ben Rosenfeld bracelet – Private collection, Photo MAW Designs Ltd

Page 143, Tom Scott necklace and ring – Private collection, Photo Jon Stokes

Pages 144, 145, Tom Scott Sketches and Photos – courtesy Tom Scott

Page 147, David Thomas brooch – Private collection, Photo Jon Stokes

Pages 148, 149, 150, David Thomas pieces – photography David Thomas

Page 151, David Thomas ring – Private collection, Photo Jon Stokes

Page 153, George Weil ring and brooch – Private collection, Photo Jon Stokes

"GOLD! GOLD! GOLD! GOLD!
BRIGHT AND YELLOW,
HARD AND COLD,
MOLTEN, GRAVEN,
HAMMERED AND ROLLED,
HEAVY TO GET AND
LIGHT TO HOLD."

Thomas Hood (1799-1845), *Gold!*

18ct yellow gold abstract brooch by Andrew Grima
(see page 84), worn by Mary Ann Wingfield

© 2021 Mary Ann Wingfield
World copyright reserved

ISBN: 978 178884 121 4

The right of Mary Ann Wingfield to be identified as the author of this work has been asserted by her in accordance with the Copyright, Designs and Patents Act 1988

All rights reserved. No part of this publication may be reproduced, stored in a retrieval system, or transmitted in any form or by any means electronic, mechanical, photocopying, recording or otherwise, without the prior permission of the publisher

British Library Cataloguing-in-Publication Data
A catalogue record for this book is available from the British Library

Every effort has been made to secure permission to reproduce the images contained within this book, and we are grateful to the individuals and institutions who have assisted in this task. Any errors are entirely unintentional, and the details should be addressed to the publisher.

Front cover: 18ct gold citrine and diamond collar pendant necklace and matching ring, Tom Scott, maker's mark TES, dated 1969 (see p143)

Back cover, from left to right: 18ct yellow gold, diamond and turquoise flower brooch, Alan Gard, maker's mark AMG, 1966 (see p70)
18ct yellow gold brooch set with 10 sapphires, five diamonds and three cultured pearls, Andrew Grima, maker's mark HJCo, 1964 (see p79)
Garnet and diamond brooch with abstract yellow gold surround, George Weil, maker's mark G. Weil, 1970s (see p153)

Printed in Belgium
for ACC Art Books Ltd., Woodbridge, Suffolk, England

www.accartbooks.com